Integrating Instruction

in

Social Studies

Strategies, Activities, Projects, Tools, and Techniques

by Imogene Forte and Sandra Schurr

Incentive Publications, Inc.
Nashville, Tennessee

Illustrated by Marta Drayton
Cover by Geoffrey Brittingham
Edited by Jan Keeling

ISBN 0-86530-320-7

PRINTED IN THE UNITED STATES OF AMERICA

TABLE OF CONTENTS

Using Integrated Instructional Strategies to Accommodate Differing Learning Styles, Abilities, and Interests

Using Multiple Intelligences as an Instructional Tool

Using Learning Stations as an Instructional Tool

Using the Read and Relate Concept as an Instructional Tool

Using Integrated Instructional Strategies to Develop Problem-solving and Higher-order Thinking Skills

Using Bloom's Taxonomy as an Instructional Tool

Using Williams' Taxonomy as an Instructional Tool

Using Investigation Cards as an Instructional Tool

Using Calendars as an Instructional Tool

Using Integrated Instructional Strategies to Promote Cooperative Learning and Group Interaction

Using Integrated Instructional Strategies to Facilitate Authentic Assessment

A Very Practical Appendix

Preface

Middle grades educators are meeting the challenges of student-centered education with new teaching methods that help create a positive learning climate. Middle grades *social studies* educators want to know how to use these new instructional strategies and organizational procedures in ways that are specifically designed for the social studies classroom.

Integrating Instruction in Social Studies was created for those social studies educators at the middle grade level. The activities, many of which emphasize current events, cover topics in each of the designated social science areas including:

- History
- Political Science/Government
- Geography
- Anthropology
- Economics
- Sociology

In each of five major sections you will find a comprehensive overview of a particular instructional focus accompanied by exciting activities that are meant to be used as well as to serve as examples.

USING INTEGRATED INSTRUCTIONAL STRATEGIES TO ACCOMMODATE DIFFERING LEARNING STYLES, ABILITIES, AND INTERESTS features guidelines for incorporating the Multiple Intelligences, Learning Stations, and Read and Relate tasks into the preparation of high-quality lesson plans and student assignments.

USING INTEGRATED INSTRUCTIONAL STRATEGIES TO DEVELOP PROBLEM-SOLVING AND HIGHER-ORDER THINKING SKILLS offers guidelines for infusing higher-order thinking skills into the educational process through the use of cognitive taxonomies, self-directed investigation cards, and calendars. The cognitive taxonomies offer great foundations for the design of interdisciplinary units, student worksheets, learning stations, and group projects.

USING INSTRUCTIONAL STRATEGIES TO PROMOTE COOPERATIVE LEARNING AND GROUP INTERACTION presents valuable collaborative processes such as Think/Pair/Share, Three-Step Interview, Circle of Knowledge, Team Learning, Round Table, and Jigsaw.

USING INTEGRATED INSTRUCTIONAL STRATEGIES TO FACILITATE AUTHENTIC ASSESSMENT shows how to effectively implement product, performance, and portfolio assessment practices. Included is a complete sample portfolio based on an interdisciplinary unit on Egypt.

Finally, **A VERY PRACTICAL APPENDIX** provides high-interest strategies and activities to integrate science, math, and language arts into the social studies curriculum; topics for student reports and journal writing; blank planning outlines to help in the creation of original lesson plans; and an annotated bibliography. A comprehensive index is invaluable in keeping this wealth of information at your fingertips.

In short, this book is a must for all social studies educators, for those on interdisciplinary teams as well as those in self-contained classrooms. It offers a collection of instructional strategies that were designed for heterogeneous groups of students in an educational setting that will allow every student to be successful. It clarifies theoretical principles and offers activities that cover a wide range of important social studies topics. Best of all, its content is fresh, original, and of interest to contemporary middle grades students.

Using Integrated Instructional Strategies to Accommodate Differing Learning Styles, Abilities, and Interests

Using Multiple Intelligences as an Instructional Tool

Howard Gardner's Theory of the Multiple Intelligences provides teachers with an excellent model for the design of interdisciplinary units, student worksheets, learning stations, and group projects. Gardner is quick to point out that (1) every student has at least one dominant intelligence (although he or she may have more than one); (2) these intelligences can all be nurtured, strengthened, and taught over time; (3) the intelligences do not exist in isolation but interface and interact with one another when completing a task; and (4) the intelligences provide teachers with seven different ways to approach the curriculum. Gardner has identified and described seven major intelligences:

VERBAL /LINGUISTIC DOMINANCE
Students strong in this type of intelligence have highly developed verbal skills, and often think in words. They do well on written assignments, enjoy reading, and are good at communicating and expressing themselves.

LOGICAL /MATHEMATICAL DOMINANCE
Students strong in this intelligence are able to think in abstractions and can handle complex concepts. They readily see patterns or relationships in ideas. They like to work with numbers and to perform mathematical operations, and they approach problem-solving exercises with the tools of logic and rational thought.

VISUAL /SPATIAL DOMINANCE
Students with this dominant intelligence think in images, symbols, colors, pictures, patterns, and shapes. They like to perform tasks that require "seeing with the mind's eye"—tasks that require them to visualize, imagine, pretend, or form images.

BODY/KINESTHETIC DOMINANCE
Students dominant in this intelligence have a strong body awareness and a sharp sense of physical movement. They communicate best through body language, physical gestures, hands-on activities, active demonstrations, and performance tasks.

MUSICAL /RHYTHMIC DOMINANCE
Students with this dominant intelligence enjoy music, rhythmic patterns, variations in tones or rhythms, and sounds. They enjoy listening to music, composing music, interpreting music, performing to music, and learning with music playing in the background.

INTERPERSONAL DOMINANCE

Students with this dominant intelligence thrive on person-to-person interactions and team activities. They are sensitive to the feelings and needs of others and are skilled team members, discussion leaders, and peer mediators

INTRAPERSONAL DOMINANCE

Students with this dominant intelligence prefer to work alone because they are self-reflective, self-motivated, and in tune with their own feelings, beliefs, strengths, and thought processes. They respond to intrinsic rather than extrinsic rewards and may demonstrate great wisdom and insight when presented with personal challenges and independent-study opportunities.

The Theory of Multiple Intelligences can be used as a guide for the teacher who is interested in creating lesson plans that address one or more of the intelligences on a daily basis. Teachers should ask themselves the following questions when attempting to develop or evaluate classroom activities using the seven intelligences.

1   What tasks require students to write, speak, or read?

2   What tasks require students to engage in problem solving, logical thought, or calculations?

3   What tasks require students to create images or visual aids and to analyze colors, textures, forms, or shapes?

4   What tasks require students to employ body motions, manipulations, or hands-on approaches to learning?

5   What tasks require students to incorporate music, rhythm, pitch, tones, or environmental sounds in their work?

6   What tasks require students to work in groups and to interact with other students?

7   What tasks require students to express personal feelings, insights, beliefs, and self-disclosing ideas?

The following pages provide the teacher with several examples of how the Multiple Intelligences have been used as an organizing structure when designing classroom materials and assignments.

U.S. History
The Civil War

VERBAL/LINGUISTIC
Write a short story in the first person about either General Ulysses S. Grant or General Robert E. Lee.

LOGICAL/MATHEMATICAL
Create a timeline of important events from 1850 to 1870. Use both diagrams and drawings to represent each event.

VISUAL/SPATIAL
Work with a partner to conduct a mock interview. One of you will be a soldier from the North or South while the other will be an interviewer from the other side. Afterwards, switch roles, switch sides, and conduct another interview.

BODY/KINESTHETIC
Create a series of physical hand or body signals that could be used as a code to send silent messages behind enemy lines.

MUSICAL/RHYTHMIC
Listen to recordings of songs from the Civil War era, including both spirituals and marches. Compose a "musical collage" of these songs or of titles or words from the songs.

INTERPERSONAL
In a special ceremony, re-enact the signing of the peace treaty by General Grant and General Lee.

INTRAPERSONAL
Write down some advice that a soldier from the Civil War might give you, a student, about dealing with Civil Rights issues in today's world.

The United States Constitution

The Power of the Constitution

VERBAL/LINGUISTIC

Write a paragraph that explains the significance of each of these in the "evolution" of the Constitution: Articles of Confederation, Constitutional Convention, Bill of Rights, Federal vs. State Powers, Separation of Powers, Constitutional Amendments.

LOGICAL/MATHEMATICAL

Make an analysis: Why has the United States Constitution endured for so many years?

VISUAL/SPATIAL

Complete each of the following tasks: (1) Construct a Constitutional timeline that shows the sequence of events in the development of the United States Constitution; and (2) Construct a diagram that shows how a bill becomes law.

BODY/KINESTHETIC

Re-enact a set of great scenarios and moments from the Constitutional Convention.

MUSICAL/RHYTHMIC

Make a tape recording of some of America's favorite patriotic songs and prepare a booklet that has the lyrics for each song.

INTERPERSONAL

Develop a series of FACT VS. OPINION statements about the development of the United States Constitution. Remember that a FACT is a statement based on documented information and an OPINION is a belief or inference that is not based on documented information. Share your FACT VS. OPINION activity with several friends and see how good they are at distinguishing one type of statement from the other.

INTRAPERSONAL

Determine how each of the first ten Amendments affects your life today. Which of these rights is most important to you and why?

Reconstruction

The Birth of Civil Rights

VERBAL/LINGUISTIC

The twelve-year period after the Civil War is known as Reconstruction. During this time, conflict emerged between members of Congress who wanted the South to accept the end of slavery and the southern states. Prepare and give a short speech, speaking as a person who wants to make sure that freed slaves are safe, are granted citizenship, and can earn a living.

LOGICAL/MATHEMATICAL

From a historical perspective, what might have happened if the South had won the Civil War?

VISUAL/SPATIAL

Create a flyer warning the public about the dangers and inequities of the Black Codes, the Ku Klux Klan, and the Jim Crow laws.

BODY/KINESTHETIC

Create and perform a drama about a group of people who moved to the South after the Civil War to help the former slaves and the suffering farmers.

MUSICAL/RHYTHMIC

Research to find out more about minstrels and minstrel shows. Organize a group of students to perform a song-and-dance minstrel show with a theme related to the Reconstruction Period

INTERPERSONAL

Create an "African-American Hall of Fame" that celebrates the many contributions and achievements of black Americans during the Reconstruction Period. Display it in your classroom.

INTRAPERSONAL

There was a total of 620,000 deaths during the Civil War. In many cases, "father fought son" and "brother fought brother." Write an essay that tells how you would have felt if members of your family had chosen different sides during the Civil War.

14

Maps
The World in Spatial Terms

VERBAL/LINGUISTIC
Examine a variety of United States or world maps, then identify and describe some basic elements of each one (include title, legend, scale, grid, meridians, directional symbols, and coordinates).

LOGICAL/MATHEMATICAL
On a U.S. or world map, measure the distance between two locations in miles and then in kilometers. Calculate the time it would take to travel by various means between these locations, and the estimated costs. Draw conclusions about different ways of measuring distance.

VISUAL/SPATIAL
Read a biography about a famous inventor, explorer, world leader, head of government, U.S. president, or historical figure. Create a series of sketches to illustrate the various settings in the story.

BODY/KINESTHETIC
Use cardboard, wood, clay, or other materials to make a model that shows a region's physical characteristics such as landform, bodies of water, and vegetation.

MUSICAL/RHYTHMIC
Plan a MAGICAL MUSICAL TOUR to visit important homes and/or concert halls of great European or United States composers. Use a map to plan your trip; include appropriate musical selections for each "stop."

INTERPERSONAL
Working with a partner, use labels on clothing, canned/packaged goods, and other consumer items to map links with locations in different regions of the country or world. Create a game, quiz show, or audiovisual display to share your combined ideas with the class.

INTRAPERSONAL
Complete each of these starter statements: (1) The most fascinating thing to me about reading a map is . . . (2) The most difficult aspect of interpreting a map for me is . . . (3) The reason I would or would not want to be a map maker is . . .

United States President

Electing a President

VERBAL/LINGUISTIC
Compile an "Election Glossary" that includes the following terms and their definitions: ballot, candidate, caucus, concession statement, convention, crossover vote, dark horse, delegate, Electoral College, electorate, incumbent, landslide, mudslinging, plank, platform, political party, poll, precinct, primary, take the stump, underdog, and whistle-stop campaign.

LOGICAL/MATHEMATICAL
Draw a flow chart or diagram showing the sequence of events that leads to the election of a president, including all the steps taken in a successful presidential campaign.

VISUAL/SPATIAL
Study the editorial pages of local newspapers and business magazines to find examples of political cartoons. Create your own political cartoon of a potential presidential candidate.

BODY/KINESTHETIC
Hold a mock election. Students may "run" for president by designing posters, creating slogans and platforms, and giving campaign speeches.

MUSICAL/RHYTHMIC
Find a recording of "Hail to the Chief" and determine why it is closely associated with every major appearance of a U.S. president before the public or Congress. How would one describe its musical qualities?

INTERPERSONAL
Working in an assigned small group, research a famous president. Share your information in a project format.

INTRAPERSONAL
Write a short essay entitled "If I Were President."

Early Empires
Maya, Aztec, and Inca

VERBAL/LINGUISTIC
Compose an ABC Report by selecting the Maya, Aztec, or Inca empire and researching a set of interesting facts, one fact for each letter. Write your ABC Fact Sheet on a long strip of shelf paper or on a sheet of drawing paper taped together and rolled up like a scroll.

LOGICAL/MATHEMATICAL
Invent a code that might have been used in one of the early empires. Use the code to write about an achievement of one of the empires.

VISUAL/SPATIAL
Draw a pictograph that shows how one or more of these empires changed the land on which they lived.

BODY/KINESTHETIC
Act out one of the following: (1) Aztecs worshipping the Sun God; (2) a city marketplace in the Mayan city of Tikal where farmers sell baskets, blankets, headdresses, jewelry, pottery, and flint tools; or (3) Incan engineers building a temple of stone blocks, moving stone up steep mountains without the help of animals or carts.

MUSICAL /RHYTHMIC
Decide on a musical selection that would best represent the movement of the sun, stars, and planets (these were studied in depth by people in the early empires, which led to the invention of the calendar). Consider several alternative pieces and give reasons for your first choice.

INTERPERSONAL
Meet with other students to discuss how archaeologists have worked to uncover the past and find artifacts that teach about the early empires. Construct one or more such "artifacts" as a group project. Consider making a pictograph, a calendar, a shield, a sword, a model bridge, a replica of a floating garden, or a piece of pottery or jewelry.

INTRAPERSONAL
Write a letter to the teacher explaining which of the three early empires is most appealing to you.

Cultures

Places and Regions

VERBAL/LINGUISTIC
Read a series of short stories, children's picture books, or novels about young people in other cultures. Describe the things that these fictional characters perceive as beautiful and valuable about their country's landscapes and/or geographic location.

LOGICAL/MATHEMATICAL
Select a major geographic location such as a mountain range, a major urban center, a coastal city, a rural plains, or a desert. Assess this place or region from the following individual points of view by recording your thoughts/ideas on paper in outline form: a homeless person, an entrepreneur, a politician, a taxi driver, a police officer, and a tourist.

VISUAL/SPATIAL
Make a collage of magazine illustrations and other photographs to show buildings, structures, landmarks, and statues that symbolize a particular city. (Some symbols are the Golden Gate Bridge of San Francisco, the Opera House in Sydney, and the Eiffel Tower in Paris.)

BODY/KINESTHETIC
Research to discover the types of physical exercise, sports, entertainment, and energy that are required for successful living and working in various parts of the world. Prepare an active demonstration of your findings.

MUSICAL/RHYTHMIC
Make a list of songs associated with specific regions of the world and identify the kinds of images such songs suggest (examples: "Waltzing Matilda" of Australia and "The Volga Boat Song" of Russia).

INTERPERSONAL
Interview someone who has lived, worked, or traveled extensively in a different part of the world. Make a list of questions you would like to ask him or her and, afterwards, write up the results of your interview.

INTRAPERSONAL
Assume you could live with a family anyplace in the world during the summer. Tell where you would want to go, and give reasons for your wishes.

The Old West

Western Movement

VERBAL/LINGUISTIC

Read a book about a western hero or outlaw such as Daniel Boone, Davy Crockett, Jim Bowie, Billy the Kid, or Wyatt Earp. Create a "magazine book report" by writing down ten facts or incidents, each on a separate piece of paper. Use a drawing or a magazine picture to illustrate each page. Make a cover and title page for your booklet.

LOGICAL/MATHEMATICAL

Early trails in the U.S. frontier constructed by Native Americans and fur trappers or traders soon became roads for wagons. Rank the following overland routes in terms of their importance to westward expansion: (1) Cumberland Road; (2) Oregon Trail; (3) Santa Fe Trail; (4) Old Spanish Trail; (5) California Trail.

VISUAL/SPATIAL

Paint a mural that shows the various stages of the expansion of the West from 1800 to 1900.

BODY/KINESTHETIC

Write a skit or play that depicts one of these well-known activities of the western movement; perform it for the class: (1) wagon train expedition; (2) stage coach trip; (3) Pony Express mail delivery; (4) steamboat ride; (5) transcontinental railroad adventure; (6) Gold Rush days.

MUSICAL/RHYTHMIC

Square dancing was a popular activity in the Old West. Find out all you can about square dance steps, calls, music, and dress. Stage a square dancing session for your class.

INTERPERSONAL

Research some important aspect of the western movement and present your information to a cooperative learning group where "each one teaches one" about the things he or she has learned.

INTRAPERSONAL

Pioneer families were often lonely because neighbors and towns might be twenty or thirty miles away from each other. Reflect on the days of the pioneers and tell what you might have done to amuse yourself had you lived during those isolated times.

Achievements of Women

Women Who Shaped World History

VERBAL/LINGUISTIC
Identify an important female in each of the following categories who was a leader in shaping the world's history: queen, nurse, author, scientist, feminist/activist, diplomat, anthropologist, pacifist, educator, world leader. Write a paragraph describing the contribution of each.

LOGICAL/MATHEMATICAL
Create a timeline that shows women who have played significant roles in shaping world history.

VISUAL/SPATIAL
Work with a group of peers to create a visual tribute that celebrates the many achievements of women in history. Determine the form the tribute will take, the symbols that will be used, and the women or roles that will be featured.

BODY/KINESTHETIC
Select a significant scene from world history that was centered around a female leader. Create a script and "role play" the incidents.

MUSICAL/RHYTHMIC
Analyze a time period during which women seemed to play important roles as composers, performers, or patrons of the musical arts. Tape a short essay about your findings, using background music to enhance your message.

INTERPERSONAL
Working in a small group, study the personal backgrounds and character traits of at least ten famous women who influenced world history in meaningful ways. Develop a project that shows some things these female leaders had in common and also shows the legacies they left to the modern world.

INTRAPERSONAL
Describe the feelings a woman might experience when leading an unpopular cause, when taking an unusual stance, or when fighting an unwelcome battle on a controversial issue.

The American Revolution

Revolutionary Times

VERBAL/LINGUISTIC

Write an essay about the issue that caused serious disagreements between the thirteen American colonies and the British government: "taxation without representation."

LOGICAL/MATHEMATICAL

Generate a "Chronology of the American Revolution" showing significant dates and events of the period from 1775 to 1783.

VISUAL/SPATIAL

Create a chart with pictorial symbols to illustrate the multiple causes of the American Revolution and the results or outcomes of that revolution.

BODY/KINESTHETIC

Re-enact one of the significant events of the American Revolution. Consider such events as: (1) the Battle of Bunker Hill; (2) the signing of Declaration of Independence; (3) the Boston Tea Party; (4) Washington at Valley Forge; (5) the publication of *Common Sense*; (6) Paul Revere's ride; (7) Patrick Henry's speech; and (8) the plight of Benedict Arnold.

MUSICAL/RHYTHMIC

Collect the music and lyrics from a number of songs that were popular during the time of the American Revolution. Analyze the lyrics and draw conclusions about the issues and feelings expressed in these lyrics.

INTERPERSONAL

Working with a group of peers, publish a mock newspaper entitled *The Revolutionary Times* to describe the many people, places, and activities of the Revolutionary War period. Be sure your newspaper contains the following items: news stories about events; feature stories about personalities; editorials about issues; and display ads about products and services.

INTRAPERSONAL

Create a "collage of feelings" that illustrates your personal perceptions about this important historical period of American history.

Using Learning Stations as an Instructional Tool

Learning Stations come in every size, shape, and color, and can be placed in ordinary or unusual locations. A learning station can be as simple as a bulletin board station that is used by students for extra credit when their regular work is done, or as sophisticated as a series of technology stations around which the entire classroom program is organized. Learning stations can be used for teaching content or practicing skills on a daily basis, weekly basis, monthly basis, or for an entire semester.

The important thing to remember about a learning station is that it is a physical area where students engage in a variety of learning activities. An effective learning station (1) includes multi-level tasks; (2) offers choices in and alternatives to the tasks it requires; (3) is attractive and motivational; (4) provides clear directions and procedures; (5) accommodates three to five students at one sitting; (6) has flexible time limitations for completion; (7) controls and coordinates movement to and from or between stations; (8) incorporates varied learning styles, modalities, and intelligences; (9) manages student participation through record-keeping strategies; and (10) encourages authentic types of assessment through the use of products and portfolios.

Some of the best formats for learning stations are:

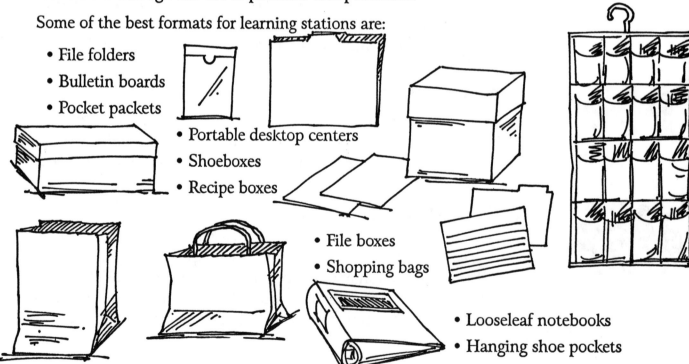

- File folders
- Bulletin boards
- Pocket packets
- Portable desktop centers
- Shoeboxes
- Recipe boxes
- File boxes
- Shopping bags
- Looseleaf notebooks
- Hanging shoe pockets

For more examples and explanations of learning station formats, see *Interdisciplinary Units and Projects for Thematic Instruction* by Imogene Forte and Sandra Schurr, Incentive Publications, 1995.

Some of the most practical ways to use space when setting up learning stations are the following:

Arrange desks in clusters of four or six.

Place an easel between two desks (or place two desks on each side of the easel).

Use bulletin boards or hanging displays in strategic positions.

Use round tables.

Place bookcases at an angle in a corner of the room, adjacent to clustered desks or round tables.

Use backs of bookcases, teacher's desk, or other large pieces of furniture.

Arrange lap boards made of masonite or plywood around a carpeted area where students can sit on the floor.

Some evaluative techniques for use with learning stations that could become products and artifacts for a portfolio are:

- Anecdotal records
- Games, quizzes, puzzles
- Logs and diaries
- Teacher- or student-made tests
- Class or individual charts, graphs
- Checklists
- Tape recordings
- Suggestion boxes
- Scrapbooks or notebooks
- Observation records
- Interviews
- Conferences
- Student rating scales
- Daily progress reports
- Library pockets with individual reporting cards

Finally, here are some things that should be considered before setting up learning stations in the middle level classroom:

1 Decide what you want to teach at each station. Write one or more student objectives. These should be things the student should do in order to show that he or she understands the concept or skill presented.

2 Decide on optional strategies, activities, and tasks for teaching those objectives.

3 Locate all supporting tools and materials for completing the assigned and/or optional tasks. Be sure that students know which materials are included in the station, how to use the materials, and how to care for them.

4 Write specific directions, procedures, and explanations for doing the work at the station. Give students an estimated timetable for completion of the station.

5 Plan for "traffic flow" in relation to other activities that will take place while the station is in use. Plan also for scheduling students into use of the stations. There are many ways to do this. Students can be scheduled to attend each station on a specific rotation. Provided there is room at a new station, students can move on to that station when they are finished with an assigned station. If the stations or station tasks are flexible and portable, students can take them to their seats. Finally, students can sign up for stations based on their interests and/or learning needs.

6 Introduce all station themes or names and the character and major content of each station before students actually begin tackling station activities. Be specific when you tell students what your expectations are in terms of their performance or achievement at each station, and be sure students understand how their achievements will be assessed. As part of this process, provide checkpoints where students may go for help should they forget or misunderstand initial instructions, or where students may review the information presented in this introduction.

Using the Read and Relate Concept as an Instructional Tool

Read and Relate activities require the student to read or review a set of important concepts in a given subject area and then use these concepts as springboards for applying a range of creative or critical thinking skills.

Using the textbook or a favorite set of alternative reference materials, the teacher begins the Read and Relate process by selecting a number of key ideas related to a topic that is being taught as part of an instructional unit. These ideas should be representative of key facts that will be learned by the student. It is also crucial that these ideas lend themselves easily to a number of extended reading, writing, or thinking exercises that can provide opportunities for students to apply the facts in a new and different context.

Once the teacher has generated a list, the concepts are written as a series of short, descriptive paragraphs to be reviewed by the student. The paragraphs should be approximately three to five sentences in length, and they should be presented in a logical or sequential manner.

Next, teachers should use Bloom's Taxonomy, Williams' Taxonomy, or any of Gardner's Multiple Intelligences as a basis for developing a follow-up reading, writing, speaking, or thinking activity for each factual paragraph. The activity should require the student to "do something" with the concept in a new and different way. The intent of this instructional strategy is to help the student understand that many important ideas learned in one subject area can be related to ideas in another subject area.

Notice how each descriptive paragraph (READ) is followed by a special application challenge for students to complete (RELATE).

Producers and Consumers

Goods and Services

READ.

There are two important elements in an economic system: business organizations (enterprises) and households (people). Businesses produce goods and services while households consume them. Things like food, furniture, CD players, and clothing are economic goods that cost money and have an economic value because they are scarce (produced in limited amounts). People who sell the food, repair the furniture, service the CD players, and clean the clothing provide economic services. They do something to or for items or people, but do not actually produce material objects.

RELATE.

Imagine that you have $1000.00 to spend on a variety of products and services for a family of homeless people that you know. What would you want to purchase and how much would each product and/or service cost? Write a letter to this "imaginary family" explaining that you are an anonymous donor who is sending them some goods and services to enrich their lives. Describe the items and give reasons for your choices.

Producers and Consumers

Economic Questions to Answer

READ.

The producers in every economic system face four basic questions in their quest to satisfy the needs and wants of consumers. These questions are:

1. What should we produce?
2. Who will produce it?
3. How much of an item should we produce?
4. To whom should we distribute or make the product available?

RELATE.

Working with a group of classmates, start a small business to provide a product or a service for members of your school, neighborhood, or community. Use the four economic questions to help you develop a business plan. Try out your plan and evaluate your results. Some business ideas to consider are:

1. Balloon Bouquet Creator
2. Button Maker
3. Party Planner
4. Coupon Book Distributor
5. Face Painter
6. Flyer Creator/Distributor
7. Homework Helper
8. Photographer
9. Mural or Portrait Painter
10. Newsletter Publisher
11. Puppet Maker
12. Rock Painter
13. Shirt Artist
14. Snack Vendor
15. Wake-Up Caller
16. Greeting Card Maker

Using Integrated Instructional Strategies to Develop Problem-solving and Higher-order Thinking Skills

Using Bloom's Taxonomy as an Instructional Tool

Bloom's Taxonomy is a well-known model for teaching critical thinking skills in any subject area. Based on the work of Benjamin Bloom, the taxonomy consists of six different thinking levels arranged in a hierarchy of difficulty.

Any student can function at each level of the taxonomy provided the content is appropriate for his or her reading ability. In order for teachers to consistently design lesson plans that incorporate all six levels, they should use the taxonomy to structure all student objectives, all information sessions, all questions, all assigned tasks, and all items on tests.

On the opposite page is a brief summary of the six taxonomy levels with a list of common student behaviors, presented as action verbs, associated with each level. When developing learning tasks and activities around Bloom's Taxonomy, it is important to include in each set at least one activity for each level of the taxonomy. Keep a copy of the Bloom's page in your lesson planning book so it will be handy when you need it.

Bloom's Taxonomy can be used to structure sets of learning tasks, student worksheets, cooperative learning group assignments, and independent study units. On the following pages you will find a collection of learning assignments based on this taxonomy. Topics were selected to be appealing to students and to blend into a middle grades curriculum.

Bloom's Taxonomy of Critical Thought

KNOWLEDGE LEVEL: Learn the information.

Sample Verbs: Define, find, follow directions, identify, know, label, list, memorize, name, quote, read, recall, recite, recognize, select, state, write.

COMPREHENSION LEVEL: Understand the information.

Sample Verbs: Account for, explain, express in other terms, give examples, give in own words, group, infer, interpret, illustrate, paraphrase, recognize, retell, show, simplify, summarize, translate.

APPLICATION LEVEL: Use the information.

Sample Verbs: Apply, compute, construct, construct using, convert (in math), demonstrate, derive, develop, discuss, generalize, interview, investigate, keep records, model, participate, perform, plan, produce, prove (in math), solve, use, utilize.

ANALYSIS LEVEL: Break the information down into its component parts.

Sample Verbs: Analyze, compare, contrast, criticize, debate, determine, diagram, differentiate, discover, draw conclusions, examine, infer, relate, search, sort, survey, take apart, uncover.

SYNTHESIS LEVEL: Put information together in new and different ways.

Sample Verbs: Build, combine, create, design, imagine, invent, make up, produce, propose, present.

EVALUATION LEVEL: Judge the information.

Sample Verbs: Assess, defend, evaluate, grade, judge, measure, perform a critique, rank, recommend, select, test, validate, verify.

Fashions, Customs

Fashion Fads

KNOWLEDGE

Define "fashion fad" as it applies to people of your age in your school.

COMPREHENSION

Name and illustrate three fashion fads popular among people of your generation.

APPLICATION

Interview your parents, teachers, and neighbors to find out what the fashion fads of their day were. Compare and contrast these to the fashion fads of your day.

SYNTHESIS

Create a brand-new fad. Describe the fashion and make a drawing of it.

ANALYSIS

Analyze the factors that contribute to the making of fashion fads. Try to determine why some are more long-lasting than others.

EVALUATION

Take a survey of your classmates to determine the most popular fad in your school. Summarize your findings in a humorous paragraph.

Helicopters

Helicopter Highlights

KNOWLEDGE

Do some research and record information about the history of helicopters and the helicopter's role in both commercial and recreational flying.

COMPREHENSION

Draw and label a diagram of a helicopter. Use the diagram to explain the helicopter's major parts and their functions.

APPLICATION

Predict new uses for helicopters in the next twenty-five years. Based on your predictions, tell how the use of helicopters may affect world communication during that period. Make a timeline to illustrate your predictions.

SYNTHESIS

Write an original science fiction story, tall tale, or mystery story about an exciting helicopter ride.

ANALYSIS

Compare and contrast the helicopter's contribution to world communication with the contributions of:

- a hot air balloon
- a jet-engine plane
- a hang glider
- a seaplane

Graph your findings.

EVALUATION

Pretend that your county government has been awarded the money to buy one of the following pieces of equipment for the use of county law enforcement officers. Assuming that you presently have none of the items, determine which one you would buy. Justify your decision with three to five reasons.

- a helicopter
- an all-terrain motor vehicle
- a twin-engine jet plane
- a high-speed automobile

Early Civilizations
Early Rome

KNOWLEDGE

Write a magazine article telling about life in ancient Rome. Include information that would allow the reader of the article to discuss this civilization knowledgeably and to pursue additional information.

COMPREHENSION

Compare and contrast the aqueducts built by early Romans to supply the city with water with Rome's present-day water-supply system.

APPLICATION

Construct a timeline to show the important events in the history of ancient Rome.

SYNTHESIS

Plan an ancient Roman feast for persons of high rank in the government. Include a multi-course menu complete with drinks and give suggestions for entertainment.

ANALYSIS

Outline a course of study that could be used to learn about the legends and mythology that formed the basis of the religion and culture of ancient Rome.

EVALUATION

Determine the importance of each of the following contributions of early Roman civilization to life in modern-day Rome:

- building of roads
- military strategy
- Greek influence on architecture, religion, dress, and theater

Cultures

Community Critique

KNOWLEDGE

Define the word "community." List some features that would provide a good quality of life for the citizens of a given community.

COMPREHENSION

Using your own words, explain what is meant by the term "community culture."

APPLICATION

Collect information about the resources in your community that offer recreational and learning activities for people of your age.

SYNTHESIS

Visualize ways that a community can be like a political party, a military force, a sports team, and/or a family.

ANALYSIS

Decide if you agree or disagree with this statement: "A community is only as strong as its leadership." Justify your position.

EVALUATION

Determine specific things that students can do to help maintain a positive climate and healthy environment for all members of the school community. Make a comparable list of student actions that can have negative influences on the school community.

Cultures/Stereotypes and Prejudices

Sitcom Signoff

Page 1

KNOWLEDGE

The television situation comedy often referred to as a "sitcom" is a product of twentieth-century culture. Write a dictionary definition of "situation comedy" as if to record the term for a future generation.

APPLICATION

Use a television guide and/or newspaper television reviews to find a "sitcom" whose characters would seem to provide the viewer with one of the following:

- an example of gender bias
- an example of family conflict
- an example of a social problem
- an example of a stereotype
- an example of relationships between people of different ages
- an example of multiculturalism
- an example of community culture

Give a brief overview of the setting, characters, and theme of the program.

COMPREHENSION

Describe how television situation comedies tend to chronicle or reflect real people, places, and events in contemporary society.

36

Sitcom Signoff

ANALYSIS

Analyze a weekly segment of a selected "sitcom" to determine the degree to which it reflects the lifestyles in your community that you would consider "average."

SYNTHESIS

Use your imagination to develop a "sitcom" character with a colorful personality and unique outlook on life. Write a proposal for funding for a TV program in which this character would star. As part of the proposal, include a synopsis of the plot, supporting characters, and setting.

EVALUATION

Develop a rating scale for evaluating negative influences of situation comedies on children and youth. Justify the ratings by stating the criteria used for your decisions.

Maps and Globes

Globe Trotting

KNOWLEDGE

After spending some time examining the globe to locate countries of the world, rank the top ten countries about which you would like to learn more.

APPLICATION

Study your globe to determine the countries through which the equator passes. List them. Ask a friend to estimate the number of countries on your list. Share the list to determine the accuracy of the estimate.

COMPREHENSION

Locate the seven continents on your globe. Identify the largest, the smallest, and the two whose shapes are the most similar.

Globe Trotting Page 2

SYNTHESIS

Use an inflated balloon to make a model of a globe. Cover the balloon with newspaper strips dripped in very thin paste. When the model is dry, paint it to show the oceans and continents, and label them.

ANALYSIS

Analyze your globe to identify:

- a country you would like to visit
- a country whose climate might be similar to that of your own country
- a country whose culture is probably very different from that of your own country
- a country whose geographical features would be similar to those of your own country

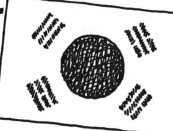

EVALUATION

Make a list of twenty questions that could be used as a study guide to help students of your age become proficient in the use of maps and globes.

The Depression
The Great Depression

KNOWLEDGE

Identify these people, places, and events that are associated with the Great Depression.

- Black Thursday
- Soup Kitchens
- Dust Bowl
- Franklin Delano Roosevelt
- Bread Lines
- Shanty Towns or Hoovervilles
- New Deal
- Civilian Conservation Corps (CCC)

COMPREHENSION

In your own words, explain what life must have been like for the one out of four Americans who were unemployed in 1932.

APPLICATION

Devise a list of questions that could be used to interview someone who lived through the Great Depression. Conduct an interview using your list as the basis for discussion.

SYNTHESIS

Pretend you were in charge of a soup kitchen or a bread line during the Great Depression. Create an original drawing or colorful description of what you would expect to see and/or hear in this setting.

ANALYSIS

Learn about the Great Depression using several different resources, including textbooks, nonfiction library books, reference books, encyclopedias, and audiovisual aides/guides. Analyze these materials and determine what you think were the major causes of the Great Depression.

EVALUATION

Judge the validity of this statement: "Franklin D. Roosevelt is one of America's five greatest presidents."

Values and Ethics

Ethically Speaking

KNOWLEDGE

Define ethical behavior in your own words.

COMPREHENSION

Explain ethics to a first-grader. Give an example to clarify your explanation.

APPLICATION

Suggest a way a student of your age might practice ethical behavior in each of the following school settings:

- during a test
- after school hours
- as a sports team member
- in a Cooperative Learning group

SYNTHESIS

Create a skit with a plot that emphasizes the plight of a person of your age involved in a situation in which behaving in an ethical manner requires courage and the risk of disfavor from other members of the group.

ANALYSIS

Take a position and write a brief paper to prove that ethical behavior is improving or declining among people in your age group.

EVALUATION

Select one person who, in your opinion, is one of the most ethical people you know. Defend your choice with at least three reasons for your selection.

Consumer Supply and Demand

On the Paper Trail

KNOWLEDGE

Develop a timeline to show in sequential order the steps in the paper making process.

COMPREHENSION

Explain the importance of paper to the field of knowledge and to the development and dissemination of information through the ages.

APPLICATION

Draw a series of three pictures to illustrate twenty commonly used products made from paper.

SYNTHESIS

Collect ten samples of paper. Devise a new use for each of the samples. (Use your imagination, but try to make the new uses practical for use by people in your own age group.)

ANALYSIS

Do some research to find the source of most of the world's wood that is used in paper manufacturing. Determine the effect of paper supply and demand on this region's labor pool and economy.

EVALUATION

Construct an alphabetical listing of at least thirty occupations that are dependent on an adequate supply of paper. Number the occupations in order of their dependency on paper. Take into account the fact that in some instances advanced technology may reduce dependency on paper.

Arts/Music

Jazz through the Ages

KNOWLEDGE

Record the important events in the development of jazz in North America and its spread in popularity to the rest of the world.

COMPREHENSION

List and define ten instruments used by jazz musicians.

APPLICATION

In fifty to one hundred words, write a brief prediction of the popularity of jazz with adults of your generation as compared to its popularity with adults of your parents' generation. Give reasons to support your prediction.

SYNTHESIS

Create a program for a jazz concert that would blend several forms of jazz and feature selections from more than one era.

ANALYSIS

Take a survey of your classmates to discover the preference of each one for ragtime, blues, Dixieland, or big band music. Use a bar graph to show your findings and share them with classmates.

EVALUATION

Construct a collage to show the sights, sounds, and scenes of the most significant jazz composers, performers, and events. Label and date the various components of the collage.

Using Williams' Taxonomy as an Instructional Tool

Williams' Taxonomy is another important model to use when teaching thinking skills. While Bloom's Taxonomy is used for teaching critical thinking skills, Williams' Taxonomy is used for teaching creative thinking skills.

Although there is a relationship between these two models, and even some overlap, it should be noted that critical thinking tends to be more reactive and vertical in nature while creative thinking tends to be more proactive and lateral in nature. Another way of saying this is that critical thinking tends to involve tasks that are logical, rational, sequential, analytical, and convergent. Creative thinking, on the other hand, tends to involve tasks that are spatial, flexible, spontaneous, analogical, and divergent. Critical thinking is "left brain" thinking while creative thinking is "right brain" thinking.

Williams' Taxonomy has eight levels, also arranged in a hierarchy, with certain types of student behavior associated with each level. The first four levels of the Williams' model are cognitive in nature while the last four levels are affective in nature.

It is strongly suggested that a teacher keep a copy of Williams' Taxonomy in the lesson plan book so that the levels and behaviors can be an integral part of most lesson plans and student assignments. On the opposite page is a brief overview of the levels in Williams' Taxonomy. Each level is accompanied by a few cue words to be used to trigger student responses to a given creative stimulus or challenge.

The following pages offer a wide variety of student worksheets, assignments, independent study guides, or group problem-solving tasks, covering many different content areas appropriate for middle grade classrooms.

Williams' Taxonomy of Creative Thought

FLUENCY

Enables the learner to generate a great many ideas, related answers, or choices in a given situation.

Sample Cue Words: Generating oodles, lots, many ideas.

FLEXIBILITY

Lets the learner change everyday objects to generate a variety of categories by taking detours and varying sizes, shapes, quantities, time limits, requirements, objectives, or dimensions in a given situation.

Sample Cue Words: Generating varied, different, alternative ideas.

ORIGINALITY

Causes the learner to seek new ideas by suggesting unusual twists to change content or by coming up with clever responses to a given situation.

Sample Cue Words: Generating unusual, unique, new ideas.

ELABORATION

Helps the learner stretch by expanding, enlarging, enriching, or embellishing possibilities that build on previous thoughts or ideas.

Sample Cue Words: Generating enriched, embellished, expanded ideas.

RISK TAKING

Enables the learner to deal with the unknown by taking chances, experimenting with new ideas, or trying new challenges.

Sample Cue Words: Experimenting with and exploring ideas.

COMPLEXITY

Permits the learner to create structure in an unstructured setting or to build a logical order in a given situation.

Sample Cue Words: Improving and explaining ideas.

CURIOSITY

Encourages the learner to follow a hunch, question alternatives, ponder outcomes, and wonder about options in a given situation.

Sample Cue Words: Pondering and questioning ideas.

IMAGINATION

Allows the learner to visualize possibilities, build images in his or her mind, picture new objects, or reach beyond the limits of the practical.

Sample Cue Words: Visualizing and fantasizing ideas.

Legal System

Learning about the Law

 FLUENCY
List as many terms that relate to laws and the legal system as you can.

 FLEXIBILITY
Write down some ways that laws affect your life, giving specific examples of each (school laws, health laws, driving laws, and others).

 ORIGINALITY
Create a brand-new law that you think would help solve the problem of teenage violence that exists in our society today.

 ELABORATION
Expand on this idea: "Law is the servant of the people."

 RISK TAKING
Describe the law(s) you have broken.

 COMPLEXITY
Try to explain why some people break the very laws that they are responsible for making or passing in the first place.

 CURIOSITY
If you could meet a brilliant trial lawyer, what questions would you want to ask him or her?

 IMAGINATION
Describe what the world would be like if there were no laws at all.

46

Jobs and Careers
Considering Careers

 FLUENCY
Create an "ABCs of Careers" dictionary by listing at least one career for each letter of the alphabet.

 FLEXIBILITY
Some career roles have been drastically changed over the years by new inventions, scientific discoveries, or the use of high-tech communication. Brainstorm a list of some career choices that were once impossible but that have recently become available or may be available in the next few years.

 ORIGINALITY
Write a role description for a career of the future in which you think you would be interested as an adult.

 ELABORATION
Write a brief description of each career that you listed in the "ABCs of Careers" dictionary.

 RISK TAKING
Determine which of these expressions best summarizes your feelings about a personal career choice: "I want to live to work" or "I want to work to live."

 COMPLEXITY
Many people look forward to two or three career choices in a working life. Explain why this is more true today than in times past.

 CURIOSITY
If you could look into a crystal ball to observe a day in the world of work twenty-five years from now, what specific career would you want to examine?

 IMAGINATION
Today most young people spend many years of preparation in school before entering the world of work. Plato suggested a system whereby young people would spend their childhood years traveling throughout the city to observe and participate in various occupations in order to help determine the most suitable. Think of an elaborate system for determining a young person's career that may never be put into practice but that would offer some benefits.

Communications

The Communications Connection

Page 1

 FLUENCY
List as many means of communication as you can think of in five minutes.

 FLEXIBILITY
Over the years, some methods of communication have become outdated and have been replaced by more modern ones. Categorize your list of means of communication into three groups: those that have remained relatively the same, those that have been updated, and those that have been replaced.

 ORIGINALITY
Early humans used pictures to communicate. Draw a pictorial report to show the history of mail delivery in the United States. Start with the Pony Express and continue on to our modern-day postal system; then add one picture to show what you think may be the next major development in mail delivery.

 ELABORATION
Agree or disagree with the following starter statement: "Due to the existence of mass media, young people of today are more apt to be tolerant of and interested in differences in habits, customs, and beliefs of citizens of other countries than their parents were at the same age." Write a paragraph to justify your position and tell how you think the source of modern communication is influencing world peace efforts.

The Communications Connection

Page 2

 RISK TAKING

One of the major means of communication in all societies is person to person. We use sight, sound, speech, and body language to express feelings, emotions, ideas, and information every day. Give examples of ways that you might communicate the following to your friends or family members without using words: joy, anger, frustration, sadness, and exhaustion.

 COMPLEXITY

Take another five minutes to add as many means of communication as you can to your original list. Compare the two parts of the list and consider which segment contains items that are most important to daily life in your own community. Did you think of the most important ones first? Did further exploration of communications help you to think of some you might have overlooked?

 CURIOSITY

Make a list of questions you would like to propose for use on a panel discussion about the future of communications with a world-famous news forecaster, a rocket scientist, a medical researcher, and a military strategist.

 IMAGINATION

Visualize yourself as the chairman of the board of directors of a major newspaper conglomerate that has subsidiaries all over the world. Create a top ten list of priorities for the policy makers to use as guidelines governing freedom of the press as it is related to privacy, censorship, journalistic integrity, and other issues that you consider important.

Cultures/Stereotypes

Peeking at Prejudice

 ## FLUENCY
List all the forms of prejudice that you have observed, read about, or heard discussed.

 ## FLEXIBILITY
Give an example of how prejudice affects the social and/or economic conditions of each of the following: (1) your school; (2) your community; and (3) your future.

 ## ORIGINALITY
Create a script for a skit to help stop one type of prejudice that you observe in your own school or community.

 ## ELABORATION
Expand on this idea and create a poster to express your feelings: "Prejudice Poisons!"

 ## RISK TAKING
Look carefully at the list of forms of prejudice that you listed under "fluency" and underline the forms of prejudice that you have observed among your classmates. Star (*) the ones that you yourself have expressed or only felt. Think about your list!

 ## COMPLEXITY
Explore your own thoughts about the following terms: (1) racial prejudice; (2) gender bias; and (3) age discrimination.

 ## CURIOSITY
If you were the recipient of a monetary grant that would enable you to enlist six of your classmates to spend the next summer vacation working against the most damaging prejudice in your community, what cause would you work for? What would be your plan of action?

 ## IMAGINATION
Write a brief essay, poem, or song about what the world would be like without prejudice.

50

Contracts

Read the Fine Print

 FLUENCY
List as many reasons as you can think of that people may draw up a contract when they are making plans to work together.

 FLEXIBILITY
Is it more essential to have contracts for some projects than it is for others? Come up with a classification system that rates projects according to the need for a contract.

 ORIGINALITY
Think of a situation that may never have required a contract but that might be improved by a written agreement.

 ELABORATION
Make a list of situations in which contracts are desirable though they may not be required.

 RISK TAKING
Tell of a time in your life when it would have been helpful to have a contract (such as when a misunderstanding caused problems).

 COMPLEXITY
Write a paragraph to explain the benefits of a contract to a person who feels a written contract is not necessary between honest persons.

 CURIOSITY
Think of questions to ask adults about their opinions of the importance of contracts.

 IMAGINATION
Think of ways that people might make agreements if written contracts were not permitted.

Arts/Music

Musing on Music

 FLUENCY
List as many different types of music as you can, past and present.

 FLEXIBILITY
Place these types of music into categories.

 ORIGINALITY
Think of an unusual way that music could be used in a child care setting such as a day care center.

 ELABORATION
Expand on this statement: "Music must take rank as the highest of the fine arts . . ."—Herbert Spencer

 RISK TAKING
Tell of a time you didn't want to admit that you liked a certain kind of music.

 COMPLEXITY
Explain why music education is often one of the first things to be eliminated when school systems are having budget problems. Tell why you do or do not think music is an important part of the curriculum.

 CURIOSITY
If you could meet any famous composer, what would you want to ask him or her?

 IMAGINATION
Describe a musical group in a primitive, pre-industrial society. Imagine what their musical instruments would be like.

52

Customs/Ceremonies

Rites of Passage

 FLUENCY
Name as many rituals or celebrations as you can think of that mark a stage in life (becoming a certain age, getting married, and others).

 FLEXIBILITY
Think of a way to classify the different rituals and celebrations of the world and classify the items in your list according to your system.

 ORIGINALITY
Think of a time in a person's life that might be quite meaningful but for which there is no traditional celebration. Design a ceremony to mark this time of life.

 ELABORATION
Study your lists and think of some reasons that ceremonies marking the same events may vary from place to place.

 RISK TAKING
Tell about a celebration or ceremony you attended that did not work out as planned.

 COMPLEXITY
Come up with a theory that explains why human beings throughout the ages have felt the need to create ceremonies to mark important occasions.

 CURIOSITY
Think of a person in another time or place who is undergoing an important rite of passage (say, a young prince or princess in ancient times who is about to be married). What questions would you like to ask him or her?

 IMAGINATION
Imagine what people would do if their government decreed they could no longer mark important occasions with ceremonies of their choice.

Geography
Country of Choice

 FLUENCY
Without looking at a map, list as many places (cities, states, provinces, geographical features) in a country you have studied as you can remember.

 FLEXIBILITY
Create a classification system for the items on your list. Your classification system may be based on looking at the places in a different way (in other words, try to go beyond classifying the places as cities, states, or other obvious categories).

 ORIGINALITY
Make up a name for a city or a mountain that does not actually exist, but that sounds as if it could be located in the country you are studying.

 ELABORATION
Use your classification system to prod your memory so you can add to your list of geographical features.

 RISK TAKING
Tell if there is anything you enjoy about studying maps.

 COMPLEXITY
Tell if you think it was easy or difficult for map makers to map all of the areas in your selected country. Give reasons for your opinion, including the nature of the terrain, the technological capabilities of the people, and other factors.

 CURIOSITY
Select a town or area in the country and think of questions you would like to ask the inhabitants of that town or area.

 IMAGINATION
Describe a journey across the country. Make it a detailed description, basing it on what you know about the country. Write your description in a one-page report.

Revolutions

Changes

 FLUENCY
List as many different revolutions as you can. Include violent revolutions, revolutions in thought, and other kinds of revolutions.

 FLEXIBILITY
Come up with a classification system for the revolutions on your list.

 ORIGINALITY
Invent a type of revolution that is not commonly discussed, but that could take place within the next twenty years. Tell how it would alter things if it did take place.

 ELABORATION
Expand on this idea: "Those who make peaceful revolution impossible will make violent revolution inevitable."—John F. Kennedy

 RISK TAKING
Tell about a time that you wanted a revolution of some kind to happen.

 COMPLEXITY
Explain why some types of revolutions *seem* to happen all at once even if they have been a long time in the making.

 CURIOSITY
Why do you think some people have positive feelings about the word revolution and some people have negative feelings?

 IMAGINATION
Pick out one revolution and think about what the world would be like if it had not taken place (or if the outcome of the revolution had been different).

Dependence on Technology

Technologically Speaking

 FLUENCY
Name as many inventions as you can that have enriched human life or made life easier or more convenient.

 FLEXIBILITY
Use your list of inventions to determine the areas of human life that have become most dependent on technology.

 ORIGINALITY
Devise a step-by-step program to help a time traveler from the past become used to life in our technology-dependent society.

 ELABORATION
Think of ways to make technology accessible to more people.

 RISK TAKING
Tell about a time when you were greatly inconvenienced because of some kind of technological breakdown.

 COMPLEXITY
Explain why some people think the development of technology has been both beneficial and harmful to human life.

 CURIOSITY
What would you like to ask adults in your life about how changes in technology have affected their lives?

 IMAGINATION
Imagine what would happen to a city whose electric power supply was cut off for two weeks.

56

Immigration
To Another Place

 FLUENCY
List as many reasons as you can that people might choose to emigrate to an unfamiliar country.

 FLEXIBILITY
Classify these reasons according to how powerful they are. In other words, what might cause people to undergo great hardships in order to emigrate to a country?

 ORIGINALITY
Make up a new word for the word "immigrant."

 ELABORATION
Expand on this statement: "We are all descended from immigrants."

 RISK TAKING
Tell if you are interested in learning about the places members of your family came from. Tell why (or why not).

 COMPLEXITY
Explain the nature of some of the problems that immigrants may have in a new country.

 CURIOSITY
What questions would you like to ask ancestors of yours who may have been immigrants?

 IMAGINATION
Create an advertisement that future settlers on another planet might use to encourage immigration.

Using Investigation Cards as an Instructional Tool

Investigation Cards provide a tool for differentiating instruction in a classroom of diverse abilities, interests, and cultures. The cards are designed around Bloom's Taxonomy of Cognitive Development, with three tasks written for each of the six levels. This makes Investigation Cards helpful in "smuggling thinking skills into the curriculum."

Investigation Cards can be used in several ways. Teachers can assign cards to students, or students can select their own cards. Teachers can require students to complete at least one card at each level of the taxonomy, or they can require students to complete cards at any given level or levels of the taxonomy. Teachers can also assign Investigation Cards to cooperative learning groups, with each group having the same set of cards, or each group working on a different set. Finally, Investigation Cards make excellent homework assignments, enrichment assignments, or assignments for students with special needs.

You will need a supply of blank 4" x 6" file cards to prepare the Investigation Cards. Make three copies of each page of graphic cards in this book. Cut apart the cards on the dotted lines and paste each one on the back of one of the 4" x 6" file cards. Then make a copy of each page of task cards, cut apart the cards on the dotted lines, and paste each task card on the back of the appropriate graphic card. If time permits, color the graphics and laminate the set of Investigation Cards for extended use. If time is limited, you may make copies of the task cards alone, cut them apart, and give each student or group of students the paper task cards for immediate use.

Students and teachers can make additional sets of Investigation Cards on topics of their choice by following these simple steps:

1 Select an object or topic of interest to you in your subject area that lends itself to the Investigation Card concept.

2 Collect information associated with your object or topic and use this information to identify major terms, background data, or major concepts related to your Investigation Card theme.

3 Write three different questions, tasks, challenges, or activities for each level of Bloom's Taxonomy using the object or topic as the springboard for ideas. The Bloom Cue Charts that are found in three Incentive Publications books—*The Definitive Middle School Guide; Tools, Treasures, and Measures;* and *Science Mindstretchers*—offer excellent guidance for this purpose.

SOCIAL STUDIES

Investigate People, Places, and Things of History

GRAPHIC CARD

SOCIAL STUDIES

Investigate People, Places, and Things of History

GRAPHIC CARD

SOCIAL STUDIES

Investigate People, Places, and Things of History

GRAPHIC CARD

SOCIAL STUDIES

Investigate People, Places, and Things of History

GRAPHIC CARD

SOCIAL STUDIES

Investigate People, Places, and Things of History

GRAPHIC CARD

SOCIAL STUDIES

Investigate People, Places, and Things of History

GRAPHIC CARD

KNOWLEDGE

Make a list of important historical figures. Try to record at least one name for each letter of the alphabet. Put each name on a separate 3" X 5" file card.

TASK CARD

Investigate People, Places, and Things of History

COMPREHENSION

Categorize in some meaningful way the individuals listed at the Knowledge level. Explain your classification system.

TASK CARD

Investigate People, Places, and Things of History

KNOWLEDGE

Make a list of historical monuments, memorials, and/or moments for each letter of the alphabet. Put each item and/or event on a 3" X 5" file card.

TASK CARD

Investigate People, Places, and Things of History

COMPREHENSION

Categorize in some meaningful way the monuments, memorials, and/or moments from the Knowledge level. Explain your classification system.

TASK CARD

Investigate People, Places, and Things of History

KNOWLEDGE

Make a list of inventions that have significantly influenced our lives. Record at least one invention for each letter of the alphabet. Put each item on a separate 3" X 5" file card.

TASK CARD

Investigate People, Places, and Things of History

COMPREHENSION

Categorize in some meaningful way the inventions listed at the Knowledge level that have influenced our lives. Explain your classification system.

TASK CARD

Investigate People, Places, and Things of History

APPLICATION

Construct a short, informative paragraph describing the accomplishments of at least five of the important people listed at the Knowledge level.

TASK CARD

Investigate People, Places, and Things of History

ANALYSIS

Compare and contrast any two individuals recorded at the Knowledge level. Show your work in chart form.

TASK CARD

Investigate People, Places, and Things of History

APPLICATION

Construct a set of fact cards outlining the important information associated with at least five of the monuments, memorials, and/or moments listed at the Knowledge level.

TASK CARD

Investigate People, Places, and Things of History

ANALYSIS

Compare and contrast any two monuments, memorials, or moments recorded at the Knowledge level. Discuss your results in a pair of descriptive passages.

TASK CARD

Investigate People, Places, and Things of History

APPLICATION

Construct a timeline showing the key dates and/or activities associated with any five of the inventions listed at the Knowledge level.

TASK CARD

Investigate People, Places, and Things of History

ANALYSIS

Compare and contrast any two inventions recorded at the Knowledge level. Show your work with a series of drawings.

TASK CARD

Investigate People, Places, and Things of History

SYNTHESIS

Design a commemorative paper plate honoring one of the individuals listed at the Knowledge level.

TASK CARD

Investigate People, Places, and Things of History

EVALUATION

Judge which of the individuals from your list at the Knowledge level has made the greatest contribution to your life. Be able to defend your choice.

TASK CARD

Investigate People, Places, and Things of History

SYNTHESIS

Design a commemorative paper stamp honoring one of the monuments, memorials, or moments listed at the Knowledge level.

TASK CARD

Investigate People, Places, and Things of History

EVALUATION

Judge which of the inventions from your list at the Knowledge level has impressed you the most. Be able to defend your choice.

TASK CARD

Investigate People, Places, and Things of History

SYNTHESIS

Design a commemorative paper flag honoring one of the inventions listed at the Knowledge level.

TASK CARD

Investigate People, Places, and Things of History

EVALUATION

Judge which of the monuments, memorials, or moments from your list at the Knowledge level would have the greatest appeal for you to visit today or revisit from the past. Be able to defend your choice.

TASK CARD

Investigate People, Places, and Things of History

SOCIAL STUDIES

Investigate the Flag of the
United States of America

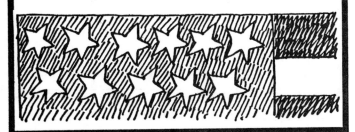

GRAPHIC CARD

SOCIAL STUDIES

Investigate the Flag of the
United States of America

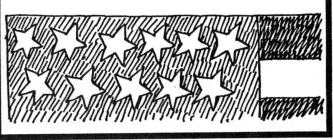

GRAPHIC CARD

SOCIAL STUDIES

Investigate the Flag of the
United States of America

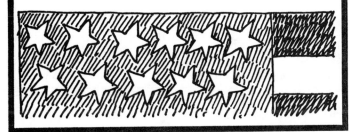

GRAPHIC CARD

SOCIAL STUDIES

Investigate the Flag of the
United States of America

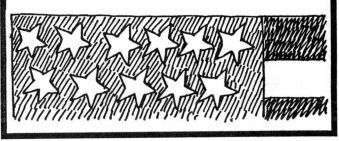

GRAPHIC CARD

SOCIAL STUDIES

Investigate the Flag of the
United States of America

GRAPHIC CARD

SOCIAL STUDIES

Investigate the Flag of the
United States of America

GRAPHIC CARD

KNOWLEDGE

Distinguish between a flag, a banner, and a coat of arms.

TASK CARD

Investigate the Flag of the United States of America

COMPREHENSION

Explain why it is important for each country to have its own national flag.

TASK CARD

Investigate the Flag of the United States of America

KNOWLEDGE

Draw a picture of a flag on its flagpole and label the following parts: halyard, hoist rope, field, fly, canton or union, staff or pole, truck, and finial.

TASK CARD

Investigate the Flag of the United States of America

COMPREHENSION

Describe the American flag in detail, giving specific information about its representative symbols and colors. Ask a friend to draw the flag according to your precise description.

TASK CARD

Investigate the Flag of the United States of America

KNOWLEDGE

Write down the pledge of allegiance and underline its key words.

TASK CARD

Investigate the Flag of the United States of America

COMPREHENSION

Explain what each of the following individuals had to do with the development of the American flag: Betsy Ross, Francis Scott Key, and President William Howard Taft.

TASK CARD

Investigate the Flag of the United States of America

APPLICATION

Locate information about the rules for the display of the American flag and present your findings in a short written report or oral speech.

TASK CARD

Investigate the Flag of the United States of America

ANALYSIS

Determine the importance of the Executive Order to Standardize the Appearance of the U.S. Flag which was issued on October 29, 1912.

TASK CARD

Investigate the Flag of the United States of America

APPLICATION

Prepare a chart, poster, or set of illustrations to show several examples of state flags with their symbols and descriptions.

TASK CARD

Investigate the Flag of the United States of America

ANALYSIS

Compare and contrast any five national flags of countries in Europe. How are they alike, and how are they different?

TASK CARD

Investigate the Flag of the United States of America

APPLICATION

Demonstrate in some way how the American flag should be handled in these situations:
a. Flag flown at half-staff
b. Flag used to cover casket
c. Flag used to unveil national monument
d. Flag used on a speaker's platform
e. Flag carried in a procession
f. Flag flown with another national flag

TASK CARD

Investigate the Flag of the United States of America

ANALYSIS

Deduce which of the following names for the American flag are most appropriate:

a. Star-Spangled Banner
b. Stars and Stripes
c. Old Glory
d. Red, White, and Blue

TASK CARD

Investigate the Flag of the United States of America

SYNTHESIS

Create a skit to show how people show disrespect for the American flag and ways to improve their attitude or behavior.

TASK CARD

Investigate the Flag of the United States of America

EVALUATION

Defend or attack this statement: "People are less patriotic today than they were a generation ago."

TASK CARD

Investigate the Flag of the United States of America

SYNTHESIS

Write a personal essay on the subject of "flags and feelings."

TASK CARD

Investigate the Flag of the United States of America

EVALUATION

The colors red, white, and blue were chosen for the American flag because of what these colors represent. Give examples of historical events and actions that support these selections.

White: purity and innocence.
Red: hardiness and valor.
Blue: vigilance, perseverance, justice.

TASK CARD

Investigate the Flag of the United States of America

SYNTHESIS

Collect a series of poems about the American flag and arrange them in an attractive display, poster, or bulletin board.

TASK CARD

Investigate the Flag of the United States of America

EVALUATION

Do you agree or disagree that these "do not" rules for uses of the flag of the United States of America are important? Justify your position.

• Do not use the flag as clothing or bedding.
• Do not use the flag as part of a costume or athletic uniform.
• Do not use the flag as a form of advertising.
• Do not use the flag as a receptacle for receiving, holding, carrying, or delivering anything.

TASK CARD

Investigate the Flag of the United States of America

SOCIAL STUDIES

Investigate the
U.S. Constitution

GRAPHIC CARD

SOCIAL STUDIES

Investigate the
U.S. Constitution

GRAPHIC CARD

SOCIAL STUDIES

Investigate the
U.S. Constitution

GRAPHIC CARD

SOCIAL STUDIES

Investigate the
U.S. Constitution

GRAPHIC CARD

SOCIAL STUDIES

Investigate the
U.S. Constitution

GRAPHIC CARD

SOCIAL STUDIES

Investigate the
U.S. Constitution

GRAPHIC CARD

KNOWLEDGE

Identify the important dates and people associated with the development of the U.S. Constitution and the Bill of Rights.

TASK CARD

Investigate the U.S. Constitution

COMPREHENSION

Explain the purpose and design of the U.S. Constitution.

TASK CARD

Investigate the U.S. Constitution

KNOWLEDGE

Record the number of Articles and Amendments to the U.S. Constitution.

TASK CARD

Investigate the U.S. Constitution

COMPREHENSION

Summarize reasons the U.S. Constitution should be studied by students in school.

TASK CARD

Investigate the U.S. Constitution

KNOWLEDGE

Write down the definitions of "constitution" from the dictionary and circle the one that relates to a study of the U.S. Constitution.

TASK CARD

Investigate the U.S. Constitution

COMPREHENSION

Describe how a person's life was different before the U.S. Constitution was developed and after it became a reality.

TASK CARD

Investigate the U.S. Constitution

APPLICATION

Construct a timeline showing the development of the Constitution from its beginning to the 26th Amendment.

TASK CARD

Investigate the U.S. Constitution

ANALYSIS

Select an amendment of your choice and determine what situations would have caused it to be enacted.

TASK CARD

Investigate the U.S. Constitution

APPLICATION

Predict what the public's reaction would be today if the 18th Amendment was still in effect.

TASK CARD

Investigate the U.S. Constitution

ANALYSIS

Determine the significance of the Bill of Rights on our lives today.

TASK CARD

Investigate the U.S. Constitution

APPLICATION

Illustrate one or more of the Bill of Rights in action.

TASK CARD

Investigate the U.S. Constitution

ANALYSIS

Compare and contrast the U.S. Constitution with the Declaration of Independence. How are they alike and how are they different?

TASK CARD

Investigate the U.S. Constitution

SYNTHESIS

Develop a Constitution and Bill of Rights for your classroom modeled after the official documents of the United States.

TASK CARD

Investigate the U.S. Constitution

EVALUATION

Look at the Bill of Rights and rank them according to their importance to you, with **1** being the most important. Explain your ranking.

TASK CARD

Investigate the U.S. Constitution

SYNTHESIS

Design a simple information booklet to inform John Q. Public about the importance and content of the U.S. Constitution.

TASK CARD

Investigate the U.S. Constitution

EVALUATION

What do you think is the greatest strength of the United States government? Defend your opinion.

TASK CARD

Investigate the U.S. Constitution

SYNTHESIS

Create a set of bookmarks based on a Bill of Rights theme.

TASK CARD

Investigate the U.S. Constitution

EVALUATION

Defend or criticize this statement:

"The U.S. Constitution is the most important document in our country's history."

TASK CARD

Investigate the U.S. Constitution

SOCIAL STUDIES

Investigate the
Generation Gap

GRAPHIC CARD

SOCIAL STUDIES

Investigate the
Generation Gap

GRAPHIC CARD

SOCIAL STUDIES

Investigate the
Generation Gap

GRAPHIC CARD

SOCIAL STUDIES

Investigate the
Generation Gap

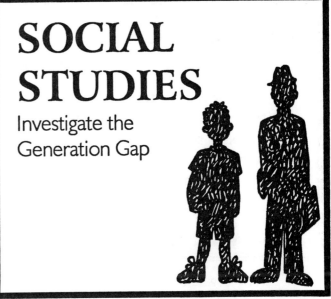

GRAPHIC CARD

SOCIAL STUDIES

Investigate the
Generation Gap

GRAPHIC CARD

SOCIAL STUDIES

Investigate the
Generation Gap

GRAPHIC CARD

KNOWLEDGE

Define the following words:
senior citizen, geriatrics,
retirement, generation, ageism,
pension, and social security.

TASK CARD

Investigate the Generation Gap

COMPREHENSION

In your own words, explain
what is meant by the
"generation gap."

TASK CARD

Investigate the Generation Gap

KNOWLEDGE

Think of five to ten senior
citizens you know and interact
with on a regular basis. Write
down their names and tell what
your relationship is to each.

TASK CARD

Investigate the Generation Gap

COMPREHENSION

Describe your favorite senior
citizen in detail and discuss
what makes him or her special.

TASK CARD

Investigate the Generation Gap

KNOWLEDGE

List characteristics that you
commonly associate with
people who are senior citizens.

TASK CARD

Investigate the Generation Gap

COMPREHENSION

Describe some of the changes
that occur as people grow older.

TASK CARD

Investigate the Generation Gap

APPLICATION

Find out what services and benefits are provided by your state or local government for the aging population.

TASK CARD

Investigate the Generation Gap

ANALYSIS

Draw conclusions about whether older people should be treated differently as they age.

TASK CARD

Investigate the Generation Gap

APPLICATION

Organize an "Adopt-A-Grandparent" program for your school.

TASK CARD

Investigate the Generation Gap

ANALYSIS

Study the things that people enjoy about being old and the things that stop some people from enjoying old age.

TASK CARD

Investigate the Generation Gap

APPLICATION

Interview a senior citizen in your school or community who serves as a volunteer. Write a list of questions to ask this individual about his or her life and volunteer work.

TASK CARD

Investigate the Generation Gap

ANALYSIS

Compare and contrast the way senior citizens are respected and treated in the United States to the ways they are treated in some other cultures.

TASK CARD

Investigate the Generation Gap

SYNTHESIS

Compose an essay entitled:

The Things That Can Be Learned
From Being a Grandchild

TASK CARD

Investigate the Generation Gap

EVALUATION

Rank the following fears that
many senior citizens have about
the aging process, with 1 being
their greatest fear and 8 being
their fear of least concern:

- poor health
- economic insecurity
- death
- loss of a loved one
- boredom
- loneliness
- inability to care for oneself
- distance from family members

TASK CARD

Investigate the Generation Gap

SYNTHESIS

Design a newspaper article
chronicling events of your life
that you would want others to
read about when you are a
senior citizen. What would it
say? What accomplishments
would it celebrate?

TASK CARD

Investigate the Generation Gap

EVALUATION

Evaluate the perceptions and
misperceptions that senior
citizens have about young
people in our society today. Be
able to defend your position.

TASK CARD

Investigate the Generation Gap

SYNTHESIS

Create a photo album or
scrapbook of magazine/
newspaper photographs that
reflect the lives and activities
of senior citizens in your
community.

TASK CARD

Investigate the Generation Gap

EVALUATION

Which of these quotations best expresses
your present attitude toward aging? Cite
supporting reasons, personal
observations, and experiences.

Who forces time is pushed back by time; who
yields to time finds time on his side.
—*The Talmud*

The more a person is able to direct his life
consciously, the more he can use time for
constructive benefits. —*Rollo May*

TASK CARD

Investigate the Generation Gap

SOCIAL STUDIES

Investigate
Ancient Greece
and Ancient Rome

GRAPHIC CARD

SOCIAL STUDIES

Investigate
Ancient Greece
and Ancient Rome

GRAPHIC CARD

SOCIAL STUDIES

Investigate
Ancient Greece
and Ancient Rome

GRAPHIC CARD

SOCIAL STUDIES

Investigate
Ancient Greece
and Ancient Rome

GRAPHIC CARD

SOCIAL STUDIES

Investigate
Ancient Greece
and Ancient Rome

GRAPHIC CARD

SOCIAL STUDIES

Investigate
Ancient Greece
and Ancient Rome

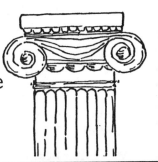

GRAPHIC CARD

KNOWLEDGE

Identify these terms associated with early Greek life:

acropolis   citizen
agora   city-state
assembly   gymnasium

TASK CARD

Investigate Ancient Greece and Ancient Rome

COMPREHENSION

Describe the lifestyle of a typical Greek household between 500 and 400 B.C. (known as the Age of Classical Greece).

TASK CARD

Investigate Ancient Greece and Ancient Rome

KNOWLEDGE

Identify these terms associated with early Roman life:

amphitheater   patrician
aqueduct   plebeian
forum   podium

TASK CARD

Investigate Ancient Greece and Ancient Rome

COMPREHENSION

Explain the concept of the "public baths" which were popular with the citizens of classical Rome.

TASK CARD

Investigate Ancient Greece and Ancient Rome

KNOWLEDGE

Define these methods of government:

monarchy   aristocracy
tyranny   oligarchy
democracy   dictatorship

TASK CARD

Investigate Ancient Greece and Ancient Rome

COMPREHENSION

In your own words, make some general statements about the clothes and fashions of the Greeks and Romans during classical times.

TASK CARD

Investigate Ancient Greece and Ancient Rome

APPLICATION

Prepare a simple outline of the following twelve Greek gods of Mount Olympus:

a. Zeus   g. Ares
b. Hera   h. Hephaestus
c. Athena   i. Aphrodite
d. Apollo   j. Poseidon
e. Artemis   k. Hestia
f. Hermes   l. Demeter

©1996 Incentive Publications, Inc., Nashville, TN.   TASK CARD

Investigate Ancient Greece and Ancient Rome

ANALYSIS

Draw conclusions about the sporting and/or entertainment needs of the Greeks, who were interested in the Olympics, and the Romans, who were interested in chariot races and gladiators.

©1996 Incentive Publications, Inc., Nashville, TN.   TASK CARD

Investigate Ancient Greece and Ancient Rome

APPLICATION

Construct a diagram, blueprint, or series of drawings showing the layout of one or more of the following items:

a. Athenian pottery
b. Greek warship
c. Greek outdoor theater
d. Roman baths
e. Roman Colosseum
f. Roman aqueduct

©1996 Incentive Publications, Inc., Nashville, TN.   TASK CARD

Investigate Ancient Greece and Ancient Rome

ANALYSIS

Compare and contrast the contributions to civilization of the ancient Romans with those of the ancient Greeks.

©1996 Incentive Publications, Inc., Nashville, TN.   TASK CARD

Investigate Ancient Greece and Ancient Rome

APPLICATION

Plan a full menu for an authentic Roman or Greek banquet, including beverages and entertainment.

©1996 Incentive Publications, Inc., Nashville, TN.   TASK CARD

Investigate Ancient Greece and Ancient Rome

ANALYSIS

Draw some conclusions about what the life of a soldier would be like in both ancient Greece and ancient Rome. Consider famous battles fought and weapons used.

©1996 Incentive Publications, Inc., Nashville, TN.   TASK CARD

Investigate Ancient Greece and Ancient Rome

SYNTHESIS

Plan and conduct an Olympics for the students in your class or your school. Research the traditions and sporting events of the Greek Olympic Games and use these as a model for your own events.

TASK CARD

Investigate Ancient Greece and Ancient Rome

EVALUATION

Judge which of the following famous Romans made the most significant contribution to their time. Give reasons for your decision.

- Julius Caesar (famous soldier/politician)
- Cicero (famous orator)
- Tacitus (famous historian)

TASK CARD

Investigate Ancient Greece and Ancient Rome

SYNTHESIS

Write an original Greek tragedy, including stories about one or more of the gods.

TASK CARD

Investigate Ancient Greece and Ancient Rome

EVALUATION

Decide which of the following famous Greek philosophers made the most significant contribution to their time. Defend your choice.

- Socrates
- Plato
- Aristotle

TASK CARD

Investigate Ancient Greece and Ancient Rome

SYNTHESIS

Create a special design for a gladiator's helmet, a flag, and a shield.

TASK CARD

Investigate Ancient Greece and Ancient Rome

EVALUATION

Evaluate the lifestyle of a typical Roman or Greek during the Classical period. Determine which lifestyle would have been the most desirable for you. Tell why.

TASK CARD

Investigate Ancient Greece and Ancient Rome

SOCIAL STUDIES

Investigate Holidays
and Celebrations

©1996 Incentive Publications, Inc., Nashville, TN. GRAPHIC CARD

SOCIAL STUDIES

Investigate Holidays
and Celebrations

©1996 Incentive Publications, Inc., Nashville, TN. GRAPHIC CARD

SOCIAL STUDIES

Investigate Holidays
and Celebrations

©1996 Incentive Publications, Inc., Nashville, TN. GRAPHIC CARD

SOCIAL STUDIES

Investigate Holidays
and Celebrations

©1996 Incentive Publications, Inc., Nashville, TN. GRAPHIC CARD

SOCIAL STUDIES

Investigate Holidays
and Celebrations

©1996 Incentive Publications, Inc., Nashville, TN. GRAPHIC CARD

SOCIAL STUDIES

Investigate Holidays
and Celebrations

©1996 Incentive Publications, Inc., Nashville, TN. GRAPHIC CARD

KNOWLEDGE

List the months of the year.
Write down a popular holiday
for each month and a lesser-
known holiday for each month.

TASK CARD

Investigate Holidays and Celebrations

COMPREHENSION

Tell about some holidays and
celebrations that take place in
other cultures.

TASK CARD

Investigate Holidays and Celebrations

KNOWLEDGE

Look up the noun "celebration"
and the verb "celebrate" in the
dictionary. Record the multiple
definitions.

TASK CARD

Investigate Holidays and Celebrations

COMPREHENSION

Estimate the number of school-
related celebrations that you
have each year and suggest
others that you might want to
have in the future.

TASK CARD

Investigate Holidays and Celebrations

KNOWLEDGE

Recall a special celebration that
you had in your family and
write about it so others can
read about it.

TASK CARD

Investigate Holidays and Celebrations

COMPREHENSION

In your own words, explain why
it is important to celebrate
special occasions, events, and
successes.

TASK CARD

Investigate Holidays and Celebrations

APPLICATION

Construct a calendar of unusual celebrations that you would like to have next year, with one official holiday designated for each month. Consider celebrations such as Baseball Month, Monster Day, Thank You America Week, National Nothing Day . . .

TASK CARD

Investigate Holidays and Celebrations

ANALYSIS

Infer which of your original holiday themes has the greatest chance for success.

TASK CARD

Investigate Holidays and Celebrations

APPLICATION

Prepare a plan for celebrating each of the new holidays by completing these tasks:
(a) Find a prose and/or poetry selection related to the holiday theme; (b) Locate a series of jokes, riddles, games, and/or crafts related to the holiday theme; (c) Prepare a booklist of related readings; (d) Prepare a bulletin board or exhibit design promoting the theme; (e) Organize a potential field trip; (f) Find recipes for holiday treats; (g) Produce a series of creative writing activities that require imagination and that are related to the holiday theme.

TASK CARD

Investigate Holidays and Celebrations

ANALYSIS

Debate the advantages and disadvantages of replacing a traditional celebration with one of your new holiday celebrations for one or more months of the year.

TASK CARD

Investigate Holidays and Celebrations

APPLICATION

Use one or more of your plans from above to produce celebrations for your class or school.

TASK CARD

Investigate Holidays and Celebrations

ANALYSIS

Survey students in the class or school to determine their perceptions of the proposed new holiday celebrations.

TASK CARD

Investigate Holidays and Celebrations

SYNTHESIS

Compose a series of reasons for one or more of the proposed new celebrations that could be used to persuade others to support your new holiday(s).

TASK CARD

Investigate Holidays and Celebrations

EVALUATION

Determine the ingredients of a successful celebration.

TASK CARD

Investigate Holidays and Celebrations

SYNTHESIS

Design a series of greeting cards for one or more of your proposed new holidays.

TASK CARD

Investigate Holidays and Celebrations

EVALUATION

Write a critique of each of the new holiday celebrations. Develop tools for measuring a celebration's success.

TASK CARD

Investigate Holidays and Celebrations

SYNTHESIS

Create a "how-to" manual for putting on special parties at holiday times.

TASK CARD

Investigate Holidays and Celebrations

EVALUATION

Make a list of recommendations to pass on to future celebration planners.

TASK CARD

Investigate Holidays and Celebrations

Using Calendars as an Instructional Tool

Contemporary calendars come in all colors, shapes, and sizes. They cover a wide range of themes and messages, often providing the user with much information for thought and motivation for action. A calendar is considered by many to be an art form and a teaching tool as well as a time management aid. Visit a book store, a gift shop, or the card section of a drug store and you will find calendars for everyone from "cat owners" and "movie buffs" to "Snoopy fans" and "nature lovers." Even museums and tourist attractions carry calendars on educational topics.

The calendars on the following pages were designed to be used as mini-interdisciplinary units. The activities were chosen to:

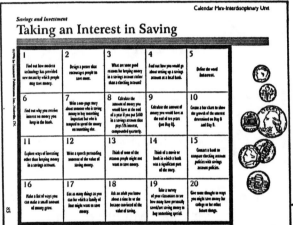

- develop skills;

- introduce new concepts;

- stimulate curiosity; and

- present challenges.

These calendar tasks can be used as:

- enrichment;

- homework;

- extra-credit assignments; or

- an addition to the traditional curriculum.

A wide variety of instructional springboards are included for each day of a typical month. Students can:

- complete each day's task as given;

- select one task to complete each week;

- be assigned a particular set of tasks by the teacher; or

- complete the tasks collaboratively with a group of peers.

One way to introduce the use of calendars as an instructional tool in the classroom is to have students bring in favorite calendars from home or solicit discarded calendars from retail outlets. Display these calendars and use them as the basis for group discussions and/or student observations. Some starter questions or tasks might be:

1 Who would buy this calendar and why?

2 What could one learn by using this calendar?

3 How are graphics, color, layout, and design used to enhance the theme and appeal of this calendar?

4 Why is a calendar considered by some people to be a "form of modern art"?

5 Why would someone want to collect calendars? What could you do with a bunch of old calendars?

6 Research the history of the calendar. Who invented it and for what purpose?

7 If you were going to create an original calendar, what theme or topic would you choose? Develop your idea into a report, a project, or a display with a calendar format.

8 What would life be like without calendars to help us keep track of time, dates, and events?

Savings and Investment

Taking an Interest in Saving

1	2	3	4	5
Find out how modern technology has provided new means by which people may save money.	Design a poster that encourages people to save more.	What are some good reasons for keeping money in a savings account rather than a checking account?	Find out how you would go about setting up a savings account at a local bank.	Define the word **interest**.
6	7	8	9	10
Find out why you receive interest on money you keep in the bank.	Write a one-page story about someone who is saving money to buy something important but who is tempted to spend the money on something else.	Calculate the amount of money you would have at the end of a year if you put $100 in a savings account that pays 5% interest, compounded quarterly.	Calculate the amount of money you would have at the end of ten years (see Day 8).	Create a bar chart to show the growth of the interest determined on Day 8 and Day 9.
11	12	13	14	15
Explore ways of investing other than keeping money in a savings account.	Write a speech persuading someone of the value of saving money.	Think of some of the reasons people might not want to save money.	Think of a movie or book in which a bank was a significant part of the story.	Contact a bank to compare checking account policies with savings account policies.
16	17	18	19	20
Make a list of ways you can make a small amount of money grow.	List as many things as you can for which a family of four might want to save money.	Ask an adult you know about a time he or she became convinced of the value of saving.	Take a survey of your classmates to see how many have personally saved/are saving money to buy something special.	Give some thought to ways you might save money for college or for other future things.

Geography

World Travelers

1 Think hard before naming the place in the world you would most like to visit. Then tell why.	**2** Name three places you could visit to see artifacts of ancient civilizations.	**3** Use a world map to locate the seven continents. Chart a course of travel that would allow you to visit all seven.
6 Research the cultural opportunities of a major city in Europe.	**7** Find out the actual flight time between your house and each of the following: Paris, France; Johannesburg, South Africa; and Auckland, New Zealand.	**8** Which continent would you visit to view the world's tallest mountain peak?
11 Create a dance or series of body movements to show the moving of a glacier. Tell three places where glaciers can be observed.	**12** Where would you go if you wanted to visit the smallest country in the world?	**13** Plan the perfect seven-day cruise to a destination of your choice.
16 Draw a picture to show a representative sample of plant and/or animal life found in desert climates.	**17** Design a travel brochure to attract tourists to one of the world's largest cities. Pick a city you would like to know more about.	**18** Research rail travel in the United States and in Europe. Compare and contrast the two systems.

4 Name the world's major oceans and tell their locations.	**5** Design the perfect suitcase for a forty-day trip around the world.
9 Write a journal entry for a day spent in the Land of the Midnight Sun.	**10** Compare and contrast any two continents.
14 Research an island of your choice and give the highlights of its physical features.	**15** Design a postcard for one of the world's major beach areas. Give the name and location of the area in your message to a friend.
19 Where in the world would be the best place to go to observe the use of high-tech systems in business and everyday life? Justify your choice.	**20** Take a survey of your classmates to determine which continent each would most like to visit. Graph your results.

Hawaiian Islands

Beautiful Hawaii

1 Name the eight major islands of Hawaii and tell about one distinguishing feature of each.	**2** Lanai, Kahoolawe, and Niihau are Hawaii's smallest islands. Write a feature article for a TV travel program telling why they are also the least explored.	**3** Rank the eight islands in terms of their attractions for tourists.
4 Develop a timeline to show the history of Hawaii.	**5** Create a travel brochure to attract tourists to vacation in Hawaii.	
6 Write a poem or a song about a Hawaiian sunset.	**7** Design the perfect souvenir for one of the millions of international travelers who visit Waikiki each year to take home.	**8** Plan the perfect day for a family of four to spend exploring the waterfalls and cliffs of Kauai.
9 Create a new recipe for a Polynesian dish that can be prepared from ingredients available in your local grocery store.	**10** Make a sketch of a Humpback Whale that you might watch on Maui.	
11 Name three activities other than whale-watching that visitors to Maui might enjoy.	**12** Plan a wardrobe for yourself for a seven-day trip to Hawaii.	**13** Compare and contrast life in Hawaii today with life there a hundred years ago.
14 Name and rank the most important industries in Hawaii today.	**15** Plan a Hawaiian Luau complete with food, dance, and decorations.	
16 Write step-by-step directions and show sketches for making a flower lei.	**17** Write journal entries including daily destinations for a five-day cruise of Hawaii's major islands.	**18** Write a myth or a folktale featuring a fictitious ancient Hawaiian family.
19 Select the island on which you would most like to spend a year as a visiting student. Tell why.	**20** Compare and contrast the states of Alaska and Hawaii according to size, population, climate, and economy.	

Women in History

Never Underestimate the Power of a Woman

1 Name five women who have made a difference in world history.	**2** Name a woman who works for good in your own community and give a brief description of her work.	**3** What was Marie Curie's major contribution to science?	**4** Why is Amelia Earhart's name known around the world?	**5** Identify three well-known woman writers and name some of their works.
6 What do you think women's roles in the military should be?	**7** Write a poem, song, or other original work in honor of the role of women in the early settlement of America.	**8** Name and tell about a woman who has devoted her life to world peace.	**9** Design an "appreciation card" for your mother or another woman who has a special meaning in your life.	**10** Find out why Cleopatra has been so well remembered.
11 Write a brief biography of a woman living today whose life story is of interest to you.	**12** Tell why Betsy Ross's name is found in American history books.	**13** Name your favorite female songwriter or vocalist and give reasons for your choice.	**14** Do you feel that women are or are not discriminated against in the workplace of today? Justify your answer.	**15** Write a character sketch of a famous woman in fiction.
16 Select a woman in a reigning royal role and research her duties and contributions.	**17** Write a journal entry of a day in the life of a woman whose work you admire.	**18** Write a letter of appreciation to a woman teacher who helped you learn and grow.	**19** Tell why you think the Mona Lisa is one of the world's best known portraits.	**20** Do you think the people of the United States will ever elect a woman president? Why or why not?

Using Integrated Instructional Strategies to Promote Cooperative Learning and Group Interaction

Using Cooperative Learning as an Instructional Tool

A cooperative learning group is an excellent means of teaching basic skills or reinforcing important concepts in any content area. Cooperative learning, as described by Johnson and Johnson (1991), involves teamwork within small groups of heterogeneous students working in a structured setting, with assigned roles, and towards a common goal. The five elements that distinguish cooperative learning from traditional group work, according to the Johnsons, are:

POSITIVE INTERDEPENDENCE
. . . requires the students to assist one another in the learning process through common goals, joint rewards, shared resources, and specified role assignments.

FACE-TO-FACE INTERACTION
. . . requires the students to actively engage in discussion, problem solving, decision making, and mutual assignment completion.

INDIVIDUAL ACCOUNTABILITY
. . . requires the student to carry through on "his or her share of the work" and to contribute as an individual to the established common goals.

INTERPERSONAL SKILLS
. . . require group members to learn and apply a range of communication and active learning skills.

GROUP PROCESSING
. . . requires the students to consistently evaluate their ability to function as a group by obtaining legitimate feedback and reinforcement.

Although roles for cooperative learning groups vary, the most common roles are those of Recorder, Time Keeper, Manager, Gopher, and Encourager.

Rules for cooperative learning groups vary too, but the most common are the following:

1 **Students assume responsibility for their own behavior.**

2 **Students are accountable for contributing to the group's work.**

3 **Students are expected to help any group member who needs it.**

4 **Students ask the teacher for help only as a last resort.**

5 **Students may not "put down" or embarrass any group member.**

The size of cooperative groups can range from pairs and trios to larger groups of four to six. It is important to keep in mind, however, that the smaller the group, the more chance there is for active participation and interaction of all group members. Groups of two, for example, can theoretically "have the floor" for fifty percent of the learning time, while groups of five can theoretically do so for only twenty percent of the learning time, if all are to contribute to the group goal in an equitable fashion. Likewise, it is important to note that groups should most often be put together in a random or arbitrary fashion so that the combination of group members varies with each task and so that group members represent a more heterogeneous type of placement. This can be done in a variety of ways ranging from "drawing names out of a hat" to having kids "count off" so those with the same numbers can be grouped together.

There are many different formats that can be used with cooperative learning groups and each of them has its advantages. On the following pages are descriptions to provide teachers with several structures that can be used in developing lesson plans around the cooperative learning method of instruction. Several applications for each of these structures can be found on pages 95 through 101.

THINK/PAIR/SHARE

In this format, the teacher gives the students a piece of information through a delivery system such as the lecturette, videotape, or transparency talk. The teacher then poses a higher-order question related to the information presented. Students are asked to reflect on the question and write down their responses after appropriate waiting time has passed. Students are then asked to turn to a partner and share responses. Teachers should prepare a plan ahead of time for ways in which students will be paired. If time allows, one pair of students may share ideas with another pair of students, making groups of four. Sufficient time for discussion and for all students to speak should be allowed. The advantages of this structure are:

- It is easy to use in large classes.

- It gives students time to reflect on course content.

- It allows students time to rehearse and embellish information before sharing with a small group or entire class.

- It fosters long-term retention of course content.

THREE-STEP INTERVIEW

In this format, the teacher presents students with information on a given topic or concept. The teacher then pairs students and asks a question about the information such as "What do you think about . . . ?" or "How would you describe . . . ?" or "Why is this important . . . ?" Each member of the pair responds to the question while the other practices active listening skills, knowing that he or she will have to speak for his or her partner at a later time. Each pair is then grouped with another pair so that each group member becomes one of four members. Person Two answers the question using the words of Person One and Person Three answers the questions using the words of Person Four. Roles are exchanged, and this process is repeated four times. The advantages of this structure are:

- It fosters important listening skills.

- It forces the student to articulate a position or response from another person's perspective.

- It presents multiple interpretations of the same information.

CIRCLE OF KNOWLEDGE

The teacher places students in groups of four to six. A Recorder (who does not participate in the brainstorming because he or she is busy writing down responses) is assigned to each group by the teacher. A question or prompt is given. Everyone takes a turn to brainstorm and respond to the question or prompt, beginning with the person to the left of the Recorder. Responses should be given by individuals around the circle, in sequence, as many times as possible within a five-minute period of time or "until the well runs dry." Group Recorders are asked to report responses from their group to the whole class without repeating an idea already shared by another group Recorder. These collective responses are written on the chalkboard or on a piece of chart paper for all to see.

- This structure is good for review and reinforcement of learned material or for introducing a new unit of study.

- It gives every student an equal opportunity to respond and participate.

- It lets a student know in advance when it is his or her turn to contribute.

- It does not judge the quality of a student's response.

- It fosters listening skills through the rule of "no repetition of the same or similar ideas in either the brainstorming or sharing processes."

TEAM LEARNING

In this cooperative learning format, the teacher places students in groups of four. Each group is given a Recording Sheet and asked to appoint a Recorder and to assign other group roles. The Recording Sheet is a "group worksheet" that contains four to six questions or tasks to be completed. A team must reach consensus on a group response for each question/task only after each member has provided input. The Recorder writes down the consensus response. When the work is finished, all team members review the group responses and sign the Recording Sheet to show they have read it, edited it, and agreed with it. These papers are collected and graded. The advantages of this structure are:

- Students build, criticize (positively), and edit one another's ideas.

- Teachers only have a few papers to grade since there is only one per group rather than one per student.

- Students collaborate on the work for a group grade rather than compete for an individual grade.

A wide variety of springboards can be used for Team Learning questions/tasks such as math manipulatives (tangrams, meter sticks, protractors), reading materials (poems, editorials, short stories), science tools (charts/graphs, rock collections, lab manuals), or social studies aids (globes, maps, compasses).

ROUND TABLE

In this cooperative learning format, the teacher forms groups of four to six members. The teacher gives each group of students a comprehensive problem to solve, an open-ended question to answer, or a complex activity to complete. Each student is asked to consider the assigned tasks and to record an individual response in writing. The key factor is that a group is given only one sheet of paper and one pencil. The sheet of paper is moved to the left around the group and, one at a time, each group member records his or her response on the sheet. No one is allowed to skip a turn. The students then determine an answer to represent the group's thinking, constructing a response that synthesizes many ideas. An optional final stage: each group shares its collective response with the whole class. The advantages of this structure are:

- It requires application of higher-order thinking skills.

- It is useful for reviewing material or practicing a skill.

- It fosters interdependence among group members.

JIGSAW

In this structure, the teacher forms home cooperative learning groups of six members and assigns each member a number from 1 to 6. Each member of a home group leaves that group to join another made up of one member of each of the other groups. The purpose of this arrangement is to have groups of students become experts on one aspect of a problem to be solved or a piece of information to be analyzed. In essence, Jigsaw is so named because it is a strategy in which each member of a given group gets only one piece of the information or problem-solving puzzle at a time. The teacher then presents each of the "expert groups" with a portion of a problem or one piece of an information paper to research, study, and acquire in-depth knowledge. Each "expert" member is responsible for mastering the content or concepts and developing a strategy for teaching it to the home team. The "expert" then returns to the home team and teaches all other members about his or her information or problem, and learns the information presented by the other group members as well. The advantages of this structure are:

- It fosters individual accountability through use of the "expert" role.

- It promotes group interdependence through "teaching and learning" processes.

- It encourages the use of high-quality communication skills through the teacher and learner roles.

Student Directions:
THINK/PAIR/SHARE

A **Think/Pair/Share** activity is designed to provide you and a partner with some "food for thought" on a given topic so that you can both write down your ideas and share your responses with each other. Follow these directions when completing the Recording Sheet.

1 Listen carefully to the information on the topic of the day presented by your teacher. Take notes on the important points.

2 Use the Recording Sheet to write down the assigned question or task as well as your response to that question or task.

3 Discuss your ideas with a partner and record something of interest he or she shared.

4 If time permits, you and your partner should share your combined ideas with another pair of students.

5 Determine why "two, three, or four heads are better than one."

A List of Possible
Think/Pair/Share
Springboards for Social Studies

AMERICAN HISTORY

1. In your own words, tell about the "first Americans."

2. Briefly describe life in the British colonies.

3. What were the early beginnings of democracy in the British colonies?

4. What are some main points of the Declaration of Independence, the Articles of Confederation, or the Monroe Doctrine?

5. Choose an important person from Revolutionary times and tell something about him or her.

6. Give a cause and effect for one or more of the following: French and Indian War, War of 1812, Mexican War, Spanish American War of 1898, World War I, and World War II.

7. What was important about the "Western Movement"?

8. Explain the "role of slavery" in the Civil War.

9. What is meant by the Civil Rights Movement?

10. In your own words, summarize what life would have been like as an immigrant during the years of 1870 to 1920.

11. Explain why so many people who lived during the Great Depression have not been able to forget it.

12. Who do you think was the greatest U.S. president and why?

13. What were some of the effects of the Industrial Revolution?

14. How has life for the average woman changed since 1900?

15. How have the major American political parties changed since their beginnings?

16. What are some disagreements among Americans over how American history should be taught?

ECONOMICS AND CONSUMERISM

1. Define economics.

2. Explain how advertising influences your buying and spending habits.

3. What is your favorite television commercial and why?

4. What advice would you give someone your age who was wanted to purchase a big-dollar item such as a skateboard, a snowboard, a bicycle, a video game, a CD player, or a computer?

5. Explain how you feel about allowances.

6. List some ways that the Yellow Pages of a telephone book make a legitimate marketplace.

7. Would you rather be in business for yourself or would you rather work for a big company? Give reasons for your answer.

8. Explain how the following types of taxation are different: income tax, sales tax, excise tax, and luxury tax.

9. Tell ways that you and your family are affected by inflation.

10. Tell the advantages and disadvantages of buying on credit.

11. Defend or criticize this statement: "Kids should be allowed to have credit cards with a parent or guardian's permission."

12. Do you agree or disagree with the position that "play is the work of children"? Explain.

13. How do you feel about the large salaries that are generally earned by the following groups of workers: doctors, athletes, CEOs of large corporations, and entertainers?

14. What makes a "good buy"?

15. How can you protect yourself against "impulse buying"?

GEOGRAPHY

1. In your own words, describe the field of geography.

2. Explain the purpose of latitude and longitude markings on a world map or a globe.

3. Cite specific examples from anywhere in the world to illustrate an environmental problem such as water pollution or ozone depletion.

4. Explain how one's physical environment has affected the way people live in a given community. Choose a community and give specific examples to support your ideas.

5. If you were writing a letter to a pen pal, how would you describe the geographic features of your community?

6. Describe the location and some of the physical characteristics of a place that is commonly in the news these days.

7. Compose five good questions that could be asked at a National Geography Bee.

8. Give three good reasons that geography is an important subject to study in school.

9. Discuss the description of a special geographical place from today's textbook chapter or assignment.

10. Explain in a few sentences the meaning of a graph, chart, map, or diagram provided by the teacher.

11. Discuss ways that the study of geography is essential or at least valuable when studying history, art, languages, and other subjects.

12. Why do some people find geography a boring subject, and what are some things that can be done to make it more interesting?

POLITICAL SCIENCE

1. Do you think there is too much or too little "government" in our lives today? Explain.

2. Explain why you would or would not want to run for political office in your community, state, or country.

3. Name the three branches of government and describe how they serve as "checks and balances" to one another.

4. Give reasons why so many 18 to 20 year olds do not exercise their right to vote.

©1996 by Incentive Publications, Inc., Nashville, TN.

5. Why do you think so many people in the United States are losing (or gaining) confidence in their government? Be specific as you respond to this question.

6. Do you think democracy is for everyone in the world? Why do you think so? Or why not?

7. What are some government services provided for you and your family?

8. What is a civil service worker? Give examples.

9. How does a bill become law?

10. What do you think is meant by the expression "lawyering of America"? Is it valid or not?

11. Define the concept of "political science."

12. Write five questions you have about the government in your community, state, or country.

WORLD HISTORY

1. In your own words, discuss the work of historians.

2. What are some interesting facts you learned about the ancient world?

3. Explain whether you would rather have been a Roman or a Greek during classical times.

4. Who were barbarians? Do we still have them today? Why not? (Or, if so, who are they?)

5. Explain the historical significance of the Crusades.

6. Do you think anything was glamorous or fascinating about life during the Middle Ages?

7. Describe the literal and figurative meanings of the term "Renaissance."

8. Give examples of both "revolution" and "independence" as they relate to your study of world history.

9. Explain what you think is meant by this statement: "History often repeats itself." Give examples to support your response.

10. Briefly describe changes in one or more of the following over time: Weapons, Farming, Transportation, Houses, Art Forms, Religion, Communications, Trade.

11. What were some outcomes of the Age of Enlightenment?

SOCIOLOGY/ANTHROPOLOGY

1. Define evolution.

2. What makes people smart?

3. Describe the work of an anthropologist.

4. In your own words, explain the meaning of culture.

5. What do you know about your ancestors?

6. What is most difficult about dealing with the social changes that are taking place in our country today?

7. Describe what is meant by the term "culture shock." When might you encounter culture shock?

8. When you compare the lives of your grandparents to your life today, what do you see as major lifestyle changes?

9. Describe how one might develop respect for a culture very different from one's own.

10. What is sociology?

Recording Sheet
Social Studies

NAME_____

DATE_____

QUESTION OR TASK TO BE COMPLETED: _____

_____
_____
_____
_____
_____
_____
_____
_____
_____
_____

MY IDEAS ON THE TOPIC: _____

_____
_____
_____
_____
_____
_____
_____
_____
_____
_____
_____
_____
_____

IDEAS SHARED BY MY PARTNER(S): _____

_____
_____
_____
_____
_____
_____
_____
_____
_____
_____
_____
_____

Student Directions:
THREE-STEP INTERVIEW

In the **Three-Step Interview** activity, you will be given some information on a topic by your teacher, then you will work with a partner to discuss your ideas on the topic. You and your partner must take turns as active listener and as active speaker. Follow these directions in completing the Recording Sheet.

1 Work with an assigned partner and decide who will be the first speaker and who will be the first listener.

2 Read the information on "Gun Control" given to you by your teacher. Think carefully about the information.

3 Use the Recording Sheet to prepare your written responses to the five questions. You will use these responses as a basis for discussing the subject with your partner.

4 After talking to your partner while he or she carefully listens to your ideas, exchange roles and let your partner give responses while you listen intently. You may want to take some notes about what he or she tells you.

5 As time permits, you and your partner are to join another pair of students and share opinions and information about gun control.

Gun Control

Background Information

INFORMATION ON GUN CONTROL

Firearms have long been a significant part of American life. They have been used as weapons in wars, as instruments for citizen soldiers, as a means for handling disputes, as tools for settling the western frontier, and as symbols of national strength. The use and misuse of guns, however, has become a major national concern, and many feel that the availability of guns has contributed to the rising rates of crime and violence. Many suggestions have been proposed for the control of guns, including:

- Registration of all guns by gun buyers, including buyer's name, address, serial number of gun, and reason for purchase.

- Application for permit to carry a gun by all potential gun buyers, including background check on buyer and wait period of from two weeks to three months for approval of permit.

- Ban on owning guns by general public.

- Mandatory prison sentences for all gun-related crimes.

The Second Amendment states:

> **A well-regulated militia, being necessary to the security of a free state, the right of the people to keep and bear arms shall not be infringed.**

This amendment lies at the heart of the gun control debate, because it is the only reference to gun possession in the Constitution. Two other popular arguments against gun control are based on the right of citizens to protect themselves from loss of individual liberties and tyrannies and the right to privacy as a potential gun buyer.

Recording Sheet, Page 1   NAME_____

Gun Control   DATE_____

Use the background information on gun control to answer these questions and to share with your partner. Be sure to record some of your partner's ideas from the sharing session as well as your own.

1. How would you explain the following statement made by a famous historian? "Guns are at the very core of the American way of life. From the first settlers to present-day soldiers, firearms have played a vital role in the nation's history."

YOUR THOUGHTS: _____
_____
_____
_____
_____
_____

YOUR PARTNER'S THOUGHTS: _____
_____
_____
_____
_____
_____

2. Which of these gun control measures has the most merit? Why?

   Option 1: Registration of all handguns
   Option 2: Application for permit and wait time
   Option 3: Ban on owning guns
   Option 4: Mandatory prison sentences for gun-related crimes

YOUR THOUGHTS: _____
_____
_____
_____
_____
_____

YOUR PARTNER'S THOUGHTS: _____
_____
_____
_____
_____
_____

Recording Sheet, Page 2

Gun Control

3. Do you feel the Second Amendment to the Constitution is a valid argument in favor of citizen ownership of guns? Explain.

YOUR THOUGHTS: _____

_____

_____

_____

_____

_____

_____

YOUR PARTNER'S THOUGHTS: _____

_____

_____

_____

_____

_____

_____

4. In your opinion, how strong are the privacy and tyranny arguments against gun control?

YOUR THOUGHTS: _____

_____

_____

_____

_____

_____

YOUR PARTNER'S THOUGHTS: _____

_____

_____

_____

_____

_____

_____

Recording Sheet, Page 3

Gun Control

5. Do you think gun control laws would actually reduce crime? Would criminals comply with these laws? Give reasons for your answers.

YOUR THOUGHTS: _____
_____
_____
_____
_____
_____
_____
_____
_____
_____
_____
_____

YOUR PARTNER'S THOUGHTS: _____
_____
_____
_____
_____
_____
_____
_____
_____
_____
_____
_____
_____

Student Directions:
CIRCLE OF KNOWLEDGE

A **Circle of Knowledge** activity provides a small group situation for brainstorming responses to a given question or prompt presented by the teacher. Follow these directions in completing the Recording Sheet.

1 Agree on a Recorder for your group. Direct the Recorder to write down the names of all group members and the assigned question or prompt in the appropriate sections of the Recording Sheet.

2 Share your responses to the question or prompt when it is your turn in the circle. Make sure you are ready to respond and that your ideas are recorded as given by the Recorder.

3 Assist the Recorder during the large-group sharing of all responses by helping him or her note which ideas have already been given by the other groups in the class and therefore should not be repeated when it is your group's turn to share.

4 Review the responses generated by both your group and the large group that have been recorded on the chalkboard, transparency, or chart paper.

5 Determine why "two, three, or four heads are better than one."

Recording Sheet

Circle of Knowledge

GROUP MEMBERS:

1. _____
2. _____
3. _____
4. _____
5. _____
6. _____

QUESTION OR PROMPT FOR BRAINSTORMING:

COLLECTIVE RESPONSES:

108

Sample Questions or Prompts for Circle of Knowledge Activities

AMERICAN HISTORY

1. Name a popular American hero from history and tell what he or she did.

2. Identify key historical dates and cite what occurred on each date.

3. Give a fact about the Western Movement (or Colonial Period, Revolutionary War Period, Civil War Period, Great Depression, or another) that seems important to you.

4. Recall a battle fought during an important period in American History and relate its outcome.

5. List contributions of African-Americans to the American Way or American Dream.

ECONOMICS OR CONSUMERISM

1. Identify as many characteristics of a market economy as you can.

2. Cite a number of examples to illustrate the Law of Supply and Demand.

3. Recall the logos, jingles, or slogans for as many magazine or television ads as you can that promote a specific company or product.

4. Identify as many economic terms as you can think of, and give a brief definition for each one identified.

5. List as many jobs as you can that are related to the health care industry (or automotive industry, entertainment industry, food industry, or other).

GEOGRAPHY

1. List major bodies of water (rivers, oceans, lakes, and seas) of the world with a one-word clue to their location.

2. Identify as many geographical terms as you can, with a brief definition for each one identified.

3. Name a place in the world and write about one of its special geographical features.

4. Give one fact about our recent study of the Rainforest (or Desert, Grassland, Tundra, Mountain Range, or other).

5. List the states in the United States and give the corresponding capital of each one.

POLITICAL SCIENCE

1. Identify as many political terms as you can think of in one of the following categories: election terms, legal terms, legislative terms, or judicial terms.

2. State the characteristics and skills that should be required of an effective political leader.

3. Give as many reasons as you can to justify a person's running for political office.

4. Generate a list of questions you would like to ask the current President of the United States (or head of some other foreign country) in a personal interview.

5. Identify as many political issues as you can that are regularly discussed in your local newspaper or on television news broadcasts.

SOCIOLOGY AND ANTHROPOLOGY

1. List as many different roles or jobs as you can that are associated with what is called "social work."

2. Give as many reasons as you can for going on an anthropological dig.

3. Using the letters from the word "anthropology," make as many words as you can.

4. Name some common prejudices or biases that people exhibit in our society.

5. List as many effects or outcomes (both positive and negative) on society and on our work or lifestyles that are a direct result of one of the following situations:

    • Reliance on computer technology

    • Invention of television

    • Hub airports for air travel

    • Globalization of the world

    • Genetic engineering

WORLD HISTORY

1. Recall a characteristic or fact of an ancient civilization that you think is worth remembering.

2. Choose a word or phrase to describe the Renaissance.

3. Name a famous world leader in the news today.

4. Cite contributions of various world cultures to the ways we live our lives in the United States today.

5. Recall a specific world event that changed the course of history.

Student Directions:
TEAM LEARNING

During a **Team Learning Activity**, your cooperative learning group will respond collectively to questions and tasks. Assign the role of Recorder to one member of your group. The Recorder should follow these directions to complete the Recording Sheet:

1 Assign one of the following jobs to each member of your group so that each person has at least one job: Timekeeper, Coordinator, Checker, and Evaluator (some members may have more than one task to perform).

2 Distribute a copy of the Recording Sheet to each group member. Ask all to read the questions and tasks.

3 Discuss your ideas for each item and reach consensus on a group response for each item. The Recorder is to write down these collaborative responses to questions and tasks. The Coordinator is to facilitate the discussion. The Timekeeper is to keep track of the time allotted for the assignment. The Checker is to read through the responses orally, checking for grammar, comprehension, and consensus errors.

4 All cooperative learning group members are to sign their names at the bottom of the Recording Sheet, indicating agreement with the responses and acknowledging fair contributions to the work.

Recording Sheet

Date_____

Foreign Languages

GROUP MEMBERS:

1. _____
2. _____
3. _____
4. _____
5. _____
6. _____

List five reasons for learning at least one foreign language at school or home.

1.

2.

3.

4.

5.

What if everyone spoke the same language? How would life be different? Would it be better or worse? Explain.

Recording Sheet

Foreign Languages

Language	% Pop.

Use an almanac to discover which languages besides English are most commonly spoken in the United States. Record the population percentage for each language listed.

As a group, decide on one foreign language that you would all most like to learn and give three reasons for your group choice.

1. _____

_____

_____

2. _____

_____

_____

3. _____

_____

_____

Signatures:

_____   _____

_____   _____

_____   _____

114

Student Directions:

ROUND TABLE

During this **Round Table** activity, you and your assigned group will criticize a magazine or newspaper article in the area of social studies by recording individual responses to a set of questions "round robin" style. Follow these directions in completing the Recording Sheet.

1 Decide on the order for recording individual responses. Who will go first, second, third, fourth, fifth, and sixth?

2 Use the Recording Sheet to write everybody's responses to both questions. After the first person writes down his or her idea, the paper is moved to the left around the group. No one is allowed to skip a turn.

3 The paper should be passed around the group twice, making certain that each member of the group responds to Question 1 only on the first round and Question 2 only on the second round.

4 One person in the group should be responsible for completing the information at the top of the Recording Sheet.

5 After both questions have been answered by all six members, the group should analyze the responses and synthesize the ideas represented for each question into a comprehensive paragraph.

Recording Sheet

Round Table

Date_____

GROUP MEMBERS:

1. _____
2. _____
3. _____
4. _____
5. _____
6. _____

TITLE OF ASSIGNED ARTICLE: _____

AUTHOR OF ARTICLE: _____

NAME OF MAGAZINE/NEWSPAPER: _____

DATE OF PUBLICATION: _____

STUDENT ONE RESPONSE

Question 1: What was the main idea of this article?

STUDENT TWO RESPONSE

Question 1: What was the main idea of this article?

STUDENT THREE RESPONSE

Question 1: What was the main idea of this article?

STUDENT FOUR RESPONSE

Question 1: What was the main idea of this article?

STUDENT FIVE RESPONSE

Question 1: What was the main idea of this article?

STUDENT SIX RESPONSE

Question 1: What was the main idea of this article?

STUDENT ONE RESPONSE

Question 2: Which fact in this article did I find to be most interesting?

STUDENT TWO RESPONSE

Question 2: Which fact in this article did I find to be most interesting?

STUDENT THREE RESPONSE

Question 2: Which fact in this article did I find to be most interesting?

STUDENT FOUR RESPONSE

Question 2: Which fact in this article did I find to be most interesting?

STUDENT FIVE RESPONSE

Question 2: Which fact in this article did I find to be most interesting?

STUDENT SIX RESPONSE

Question 2: Which fact in this article did I find to be most interesting?

Student Directions:
JIGSAW ACTIVITY

During the **Jigsaw Activity** you will work in a group of six in order to learn something new about Japan, and then teach this information to members of your home group. Follow these directions in order to complete the Recording Sheet.

1 Assign a number from one through six to each member of your home group.

2 With the help of your teacher, give each member of your group his or her appropriately numbered paragraph describing some important aspect of Japan on the next page. Don't let anyone see any paragraph but his or her own.

3 When the teacher gives you the signal, locate the other people in small home groups in your classroom who have a number the same as yours. Meet with them and together learn the information discussed in your paragraph so that each of you becomes an "expert" on its content. Once you have learned this information, have the group decide on a strategy for teaching it to the other members of your home group.

4 Return to your home team and teach all of the other members about your paragraph. Learn the information presented by them in their assigned paragraphs as well.

120

Recording Sheet

Japan

Date_____

HOME GROUP MEMBERS:

STUDENT **1** _____

STUDENT **2** _____

STUDENT **3** _____

STUDENT **4** _____

STUDENT **5** _____

STUDENT **6** _____

Cut apart the paragraphs about Japan. Give each section to the appropriate person in your group. Meet with the other students in the class who have a number that is the same as yours and learn the information discussed in the paragraph.

STUDENT **1** **Introduction to Japan**

Japan is actually a chain of 4000 islands housing almost 123 million people. These islands are called Honshu, Hokkaido, Kyushu, and Hikoku. Most of Japan is covered by mountains and forests with very few rivers, but many large lakes. Japan has a history of earthquakes and, in the summer, typhoons. The Japanese refer to their country as "Nippon," and they believed at one time that their country was created by "tears from heaven."

STUDENT **2** **Tokyo**

Tokyo is the capital and largest city of Japan. It is the center of Japanese government, business, broadcasting, and news. The city suffers from urban sprawl as it merges with surrounding towns across the Kanto plain. At one time, Tokyo was a small fishing village. The warlord Tokugawa built the great Edo Castle there about 400 years ago, making it the center of power in Japan. About 100 years ago the emperor Jeiji moved from Kyoto to Edo and renamed it Tokyo, which means "Eastern Capital."

121

STUDENT 3 Population

Japan is one of the most densely populated countries in the world. There are 847 people for every square mile in Japan. Compare this to Canada's fewer than 8 people per square mile. Most of Japan's people live in towns and cities. There are eleven cities that have populations of more than a million. There are people living on about 440 of the nearly 4000 islands of Japan.

STUDENT 4 Industries of Japan

Japan is one of the world's most powerful trading nations, though it has few natural resources and must import most of its raw materials. Japan builds more ships than any other country in the world. It produces 10 million cars and 5 million motorcycles each year and is a world leader in the production of such consumer items as calculators, pianos, radios, television sets, watches, and washing machines. Japan is also a great fishing nation: over 10 million tons of fish are caught each year.

STUDENT 5 Mount Fuji

Mount Fuji is the largest and best-known mountain in Japan. It contains an inactive volcano which last erupted in 1707, scattering ash as far away as Tokyo. It is amazingly symmetrical and it is often drawn or painted by Japanese artists. Mount Fuji is a national park, and people are allowed to climb the mountain in July and August. The top is covered with snow the rest of the year.

STUDENT 6 Religion and Education

Japan has two main religions. The oldest, Shinto, is unique to Japan and is based on respect for nature. The other is Buddhism, which originated in India and came to Japan through China. Buddhists value the duty of kindness to all living things. Most Japanese people practice both religions. All children go to primary school and then junior high school. Most Japanese go to high school, and more than a third go to a university. Children in school wear uniforms and spend long days and evenings in school, including Saturdays.

Using Integrated Instructional Strategies to Facilitate Authentic Assessment

An Overview of Authentic Assessment

In comparison with traditional types of assessment, assessment practices today emphasize more authentic ways to demonstrate that student learning has taken place. There is less assessment of the recall of information and more of the processing of information. Collecting evidence about a student over time in realistic settings is the best way to document growth and acquisition of both skills and content.

Product, performance, and portfolio assessment offer alternative assessment methods. They are all more authentic than traditional methods because they:

- require collaboration among student, teacher, and peers;
- encourage student ownership through self-assessment;
- set flexible time limits;
- are scored through multi-faceted systems;
- allow for student strengths and weaknesses;
- make use of individual learning styles and interests; and
- minimize competition.

In short, authentic assessment is designed to reflect real-world applications of knowledge whenever possible.

PRODUCT ASSESSMENT
. . . requires the student to produce a concrete end result. This can take many forms, ranging from a videotape or experiment to an exhibit or report.

PERFORMANCE ASSESSMENT
. . . requires the student to actively demonstrate a set of skills and processes while performing a predetermined task.

PORTFOLIO ASSESSMENT
. . . requires the student to maintain a collection of artifacts that reflects the student's overall efforts, progress, and achievements in one or more areas. It is important to note that both products and performances can and should become artifacts contained within the portfolio itself.

Assessment is also made more authentic through the consistent use of rubrics and metacognitive reflections throughout the assessment experience.

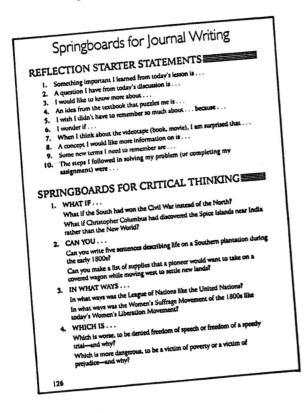

Springboards for Journal Writing

REFLECTION STARTER STATEMENTS

1. Something important I learned from today's lesson is . . .
2. A question I have from today's discussion is . . .
3. I would like to know more about . . .
4. An idea from the textbook that puzzles me is . . .
5. I wish I didn't have to remember so much about . . . because . . .
6. I wonder if . . .
7. When I think about the videotape (book, movie), I am surprised that . . .
8. A concept I would like more information on is . . .
9. Some new terms I need to remember are . . .
10. The steps I followed in solving my problem (or completing my assignment) were . . .

SPRINGBOARDS FOR CRITICAL THINKING

1. WHAT IF . . .
   What if the South had won the Civil War instead of the North?
   What if Christopher Columbus had discovered the Spice Islands near India rather than the New World?

2. CAN YOU . . .
   Can you write five sentences describing life on a Southern plantation during the early 1800s?
   Can you make a list of supplies that a pioneer would want to take on a covered wagon while moving west to settle new lands?

3. IN WHAT WAYS . . .
   In what ways was the League of Nations like the United Nations?
   In what ways was the Women's Suffrage Movement of the 1800s like today's Women's Liberation Movement?

4. WHICH IS . . .
   Which is worse, to be denied freedom of speech or freedom of a speedy trial—and why?
   Which is more dangerous, to be a victim of poverty or a victim of prejudice—and why?

126

Rubrics are checklists that contain sets of criteria for measuring the elements of a product, performance, or portfolio. They can be designed as a qualitative measure (holistic rubric) to gauge overall performance to a prompt, or they can be designed as a quantitative measure (analytic rubric) to award points for each of several elements in a response to a prompt.

Metacognitive reflections are self-assessment observations and statements made by the individual student about each product or performance that he or she has completed. These reflections become part of the portfolio contents.

Although authentic assessment is designed to enhance and support the curriculum rather than dictate or limit the curriculum, it should be noted that more traditional types of measurements such as paper/pencil quizzes, objective end-of-chapter tests, and standardized achievement exams continue to play an important role in today's assessment practices. They should become one type of artifact included in the portfolio or one type of grade assigned to a performance or one type of measure used to determine the value of a product.

The following pages of this section provide the reader with a sample portfolio in social studies for a typical middle level student. This prototype is intended to show how authentic assessment—in the form of product, performance, and portfolio samples—can be used effectively to document student growth and achievement over time. It also contains student reflections and self-assessments that are intended to realistically appraise how the student is doing based on his or her own judgment in collaboration with the judgment of others, including the teacher.

Springboards for Journal Writing

REFLECTION STARTER STATEMENTS

1. Something important I learned from today's lesson is . . .
2. A question I have from today's discussion is . . .
3. I would like to know more about . . .
4. An idea from the textbook that puzzles me is . . .
5. I wish I didn't have to remember so much about . . . because . . .
6. I wonder if . . .
7. When I think about the videotape (book, movie), I am surprised that . . .
8. A concept I would like more information on is . . .
9. Some new terms I need to remember are . . .
10. The steps I followed in solving my problem (or completing my assignment) were . . .

SPRINGBOARDS FOR CRITICAL THINKING

1. **WHAT IF . . .**

   What if the South had won the Civil War instead of the North?

   What if Christopher Columbus had discovered the Spice Islands near India rather than the New World?

2. **CAN YOU . . .**

   Can you write five sentences describing life on a Southern plantation during the early 1800s?

   Can you make a list of supplies that a pioneer would want to take on a covered wagon while moving west to settle new lands?

3. **IN WHAT WAYS . . .**

   In what ways was the League of Nations like the United Nations?

   In what ways was the Women's Suffrage Movement of the 1800s like today's Women's Liberation Movement?

4. **WHICH IS . . .**

   Which is worse, to be denied freedom of speech or freedom of a speedy trial—and why?

   Which is more dangerous, to be a victim of poverty or a victim of prejudice—and why?

SPRINGBOARDS FOR CREATIVE THINKING ≡≡≡≡

1. **YOU ARE AN ADVISOR.**

   What advice would you give today's First Lady of the United States?

   What advice would you give Napoleon if he were alive today?

2. **YOU ARE AN IMPROVER.**

   How would you reduce the impact of television on today's youth?

   How would you increase the percentage of 18-year-olds voting in local, state, and national elections?

3. **YOU ARE A DESIGNER.**

   Design a new currency system for your country.

   Create a new design for a modern peace symbol.

4. **YOU ARE A WORD SPECIALIST.**

   List all of the words you can think of that describe life during the Great Depression.

   Write down all of the words you can make from the letters in the word CONSTITUTION.

5. **YOU ARE A DISCOVERER.**

   You are an Egyptian scribe who has just discovered the English alphabet. What do you do?

   You are Ponce de Leon and have just landed on the shores of Florida. What do you see and what do you think?

6. **YOU ARE AN OBSERVER.**

   You are one of the first passengers on the Transcontinental Railroad. What things do you see, feel, and hear as the train pulls out of the station to go from the east coast to Sacramento, California?

   You are one of the fifty-five delegates who met in Philadelphia in May of 1787 and decided to write a new Constitution. Describe your observations, feelings, and memories of this historic event.

7. **YOU ARE A WRITER.**

   Write a thank-you note to Francis Scott Key for creating the words to our national anthem, "The Star-Spangled Banner."

   Compose a letter from one brother to another who fought on the opposite side during the Civil War.

SPRINGBOARDS BASED ON BLOOM'S TAXONOMY ≡

KNOWLEDGE LEVEL JOURNAL ENTRIES

a. Record the who, what, when, where, why, and how of one of the following events: Pony Express, Alamo, Gadsden Purchase, or the Gold Rush.

b. Locate and define five to ten important terms associated with geography, economics, or anthropology.

COMPREHENSION LEVEL JOURNAL ENTRIES

a. Summarize the contribution of any one of the following European explorers who discovered a part of the New World: Juan Ponce de Leon, Giovanni da Verrazano, Hernando DeSoto, Francisco de Coronado, Juan Rodriguez Cabrillo, Samuel de Champlain, or Henry Hudson.

b. Give an example from American or World History to illustrate one of the following concepts: economic revolution, political revolution, social revolution, anthropological revolution.

APPLICATION LEVEL JOURNAL ENTRIES

a. Discuss reasons that older people of today who lived through the Depression can never forget it. Make a list of questions you might ask someone who lived during this time.

b. Organize a panel discussion on a social studies topic of your choice. Make a list of important ideas to include as part of this discussion.

ANALYSIS LEVEL JOURNAL ENTRIES

a. Debate the pros and cons of tightening our immigration laws. Try to list at least three pros and three cons to use in preparing for this debate.

b. First write down some questions to include on a survey to determine perceptions of the causes and effects of the changing American family. Then survey members of your class or school.

SYNTHESIS LEVEL JOURNAL ENTRIES

a. Imagine what life would be like in one of the following situations: a society free of prejudice; a society free of crime; a society free of poverty; a society free of ignorance; a society free of propaganda.

b. Invent a political party. Name it, describe it, and formulate a platform for it.

EVALUATION LEVEL JOURNAL ENTRIES

a. Support or criticize this Chinese proverb: "With time and patience, the mulberry leaf becomes a silk gown."

b. Defend the wisdom of this Native American proverb: "Never criticize a man until you've walked a mile in his moccasins."

Springboards for Student Products

1. Create a collage, poster, montage, or display to answer one of the following questions:

    > WHAT IS HISTORY?
    > WHAT IS GEOGRAPHY?
    > WHAT IS ECONOMICS?
    > WHAT IS ANTHROPOLOGY?
    > WHAT IS SOCIOLOGY?
    > WHAT IS SOCIAL STUDIES?

2. Construct an interesting timeline that shows the historical evolution for a given country or world society on any one of the following topics: art, buildings, transportation, food and farming, people, religion, fads and fashions, communication, technology, or trade and money.

3. Write and illustrate an article for a fictitious magazine entitled "Sung and Unsung Heroes of the Past." Write about someone who lived during the Classical Ages of Rome and Greece, the Middle Ages, or the Renaissance period in history.

4. Prepare a "Who's Who" of important people associated with one of these wars: American Revolutionary War, American Civil War, World War I, or World War II.

5. Construct a drawing or model of one of the following: a slave ship, a Conestoga wagon, a stage coach, or an iron horse.

6. Invent a board game, card game, word game, or jeopardy game on a social studies topic of your choice. Include playing pieces, directions, and packaging specifications for your game.

7. Design a bulletin board depicting famous Native Americans, Hispanic Americans, African Americans, or Asian Americans.

8. Compile a photo essay to show the special geographic features and natural resources of your community or city.

9. Create a wall mural depicting the many different freedoms protected by the United States Constitution and the Bill of Rights.

10. Plan and tape record an interview between you and one of the individuals listed below. Prepare a list of questions you would like to ask him or her for this purpose.

   - **Interview a senior citizen to determine "how life differs from one generation to the next."**

   - **Interview a politician to determine the most important social, economic, and political issues that are facing your community at the present time.**

   - **Interview a businessperson to determine which job skills are most important in the hiring of an employee today.**

   - **Interview a religious leader to determine the role of the church in a changing society.**

   - **Interview a health care worker to determine the role of ethics in medicine today.**

   - **Interview a social worker to determine the special needs of individuals in today's complex world.**

11. Select one of these ideas to design a set of postcards to illustrate a social studies topic.

   - **A set of postcards depicting life of the Pilgrims, the pioneers, the colonists, the western frontier, the Gold Rush days, or the plantation owners of the South.**

   - **A set of postcards showing the most important flora and fauna found in your state.**

   - **A set of postcards showing the different ways that people make a living in your community.**

   - **A set of postcards highlighting ways that man has altered the environment in today's society.**

   Create illustrations, pictures, drawings, or diagrams for one side of each card and write an appropriate message sharing interesting facts or statistics on the other side of each card.

12. Create a billboard that teaches others an important concept from your study of history, geography, economics, or politics.

Springboards for Performances

1. Plan and deliver a "how-to" presentation that demonstrates one of the following skills:

    How to Use a Globe

    How to Use a Map

    How to Use a Compass

    How to Use an Atlas

2. Write a script for a "role play" of a scene from the book *Robinson Crusoe*. The fictional character Crusoe survived on a desert island for many years until he was rescued by the crew of a passing ship. Show how this character used the natural resources and/or geographical features of the island to survive.

3. Organize and stage a debate with three other classmates to decide whether it would be in the best interests of Mexico, Canada, and the United States to become one large country and eliminate borders and border guards.

4. Prepare and deliver a three-minute speech on one of the topics listed below. Give specific examples to support your ideas.

    Our "Shrinking" Globe or World

    Our "Shrinking" Dollar or Budget

    Our "Shrinking" Institutions or Organizations

    Our "Shrinking" Values and Ethics

    Our "Shrinking" Families and Neighborhoods

    Our "Shrinking" Opportunities and Incentives

5. Collect a number of articles on a current topic of special interest to you. Present your news in one of the following formats: a tape-recorded radio show, a videotaped television news broadcast, a printed newspaper that can be circulated.

6. Write and deliver a tribute to a local group or organization that has played a part in serving the social, economic, or political needs of selected people in your community.

7. Organize and lead a protest march to lodge a legitimate but peaceful complaint against society. To do this activity, you should:

- gather people who have a similar complaint and share your ideas with one another;

- obtain approval to act as spokesperson for the group;

- design placards that announce your complaint;

- choose a day and place for the march to take place;

- advertise the march so that other interested persons can join it or support you;

- design booklets describing your complaint to hand out to observers of your march.

8. Plan and implement one of the following challenges:

- a booth for a foreign country at an International Fair

- a display for a historical museum

- a business enterprise where you produce a product or provide a service for a classroom/school marketplace

- a mock archaeological dig for an imaginary culture

- an election for a classroom/school office

- a mock trial based on a popular fairy tale

9. Compose a series of couplets that will help you remember facts from a social studies unit, and practice reciting the couplets to the class.

10. Turn a current event into a tall tale and tell your story to the class.

11. Select a picture book that tells a story about another culture. Practice reading it aloud. Use the book to conduct a story-telling session for a group of younger students.

12. Prepare a "chalk talk" or picture essay on the blackboard about a social studies topic of your choice. Be sure to include five to ten symbols in your report to illustrate key facts or points you want to discuss with the audience.

SAMPLE PORTFOLIO FOR MIDDLE GRADES SOCIAL STUDIES

MY PORTFOLIO:

Interdisciplinary Unit on Egypt

TABLE OF CONTENTS

MATHEMATICS ARTIFACT SELECTIONS

1. Measurement Chart Using Egyptian Cubit Concept

2. Simple Math Problems Using Egyptian Symbols

SCIENCE ARTIFACT SELECTION

Making Paper (Egyptian Papyrus)

ART ARTIFACT SELECTIONS

1. Frieze of Scenes Depicting Life of a Pharaoh

2. Construction of a Paddle Doll

LANGUAGE ARTS ARTIFACTS

Two Reviews of Picture Books about Egypt

SOCIAL STUDIES ARTIFACT SELECTIONS

1. Map of Ancient Egypt
2. Timeline of Ancient Egypt

ASSESSMENT TOOLS FOR ARTIFACTS

My Portfolio Rubric/Conference Questions

Measurement Chart

Egyptian Cubit Concept

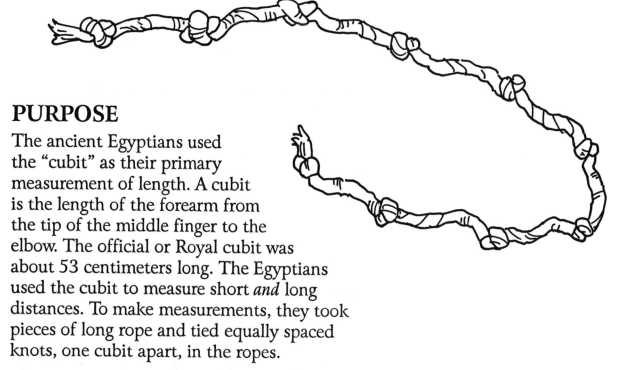

PURPOSE

The ancient Egyptians used the "cubit" as their primary measurement of length. A cubit is the length of the forearm from the tip of the middle finger to the elbow. The official or Royal cubit was about 53 centimeters long. The Egyptians used the cubit to measure short *and* long distances. To make measurements, they took pieces of long rope and tied equally spaced knots, one cubit apart, in the ropes.

WHAT I DID

I acquired a thin rope of 3 meters in length. Beginning at one end of the rope, I measured off a cubit, then tied a knot at that point. I continued to measure cubits and tie knots until I ran out of rope. I made sure that my cubit measurements were equally spaced. Next, I used my rope to measure various distances in and around my classroom, school, and playground. On a large piece of posterboard, I made a chart of all the distances measured, showing the number of cubits for each measurement. I recorded 20 different measurements on my chart. My teacher has my poster displayed on the bulletin board.

Reflection:

I worked with two friends on this project and we discovered that the length of a cubit can vary because arms and fingers vary in length. It was lots of fun measuring things with the rope, easier than measuring things with a meter stick. The hardest part for me was tying the knots so that they were equal in size and of equal distance apart.

Using Egyptian Symbols

Simple Math Problems

PURPOSE

The Egyptians used mathematical symbols that are very different from the ones we use, and they worked their math problems in a way that might seem funny to us. From our point of view, they did it backwards! They wrote their numbers with the ones written on the left, followed on the right by tens, hundreds, thousands, ten thousands, hundred thousands, and millions.

WHAT I DID

I used the following Egyptian math symbols to both translate Egyptian symbols into numbers and to write numbers Egyptian style. I did all of my work with these Egyptian symbols on a "scroll" that I made, and tied the whole thing with a colored ribbon. Because the scroll is too bulky for my portfolio, I have included some samples of my work on this page. If you would like to see my scroll, it is stored in my portfolio file box.

Name of Symbol	Egyptian Symbol	Hindu-Arabic Symbol
Tally	❘	1
Heel Bone	∩	10
Coil of Rope	୨	100
Lotus Flower	⋈	1,000
Bent Stick	⌐	10,000
Fish	⪥	100,000
Astonished Man	⨂	1,000,000

Math Problems

$307 = $ ❘❘❘❘❘❘❘୨୨୨

$2,200,002 = $ ❘❘ ⋈⋈ ⨂⨂

$63 = $ ❘❘❘∩∩∩∩∩∩

$100,055 = $ ❘❘❘❘❘∩∩∩∩∩⪥

$32 + 28 = $ ∩∩∩∩∩∩

$105 - 73 = $ ❘❘∩∩∩

❘∩୨+∩∩⨂ $ = $ ❘∩∩∩୨⨂

Reflection:

This project was much more difficult than it looks because I am used to writing numbers my way. I even tried writing some fractions using Egyptian numbers, but I found it to be impossible. I'm glad I never went to school in ancient Egypt. I would have flunked math. I think kids who are artistic might be better at Egyptian math than kids who aren't, because the numbers are more like drawings than numerals. Since I like to draw, I could at least form the Egyptian symbols pretty well, even if I couldn't figure out the math problems very well.

Papyrus

Making Paper

PURPOSE

Papyrus is a tall reed that grows in the marshes and shallow waters along the banks of the Nile River in Egypt. It was used by the Egyptians for making everything from baskets and floor mats to paper and pens. Paper was made from papyrus by peeling away the outer covering of the reed and slicing the center of the reed (called the pith) into very thin slices. These slices were then placed across each other and beaten together with a mallet. The paper was smoothed with a polishing stone. The pens were made from sharpened reeds, and the ink from the soot of the reeds.

WHAT I DID

In science class we worked in teams, spending a week making paper. Here are the steps we followed to make recycled paper.

1 We tore pieces of newsprint into small pieces and soaked them in a bowl of water overnight.

2 The next day we used an electric hand mixer to beat the soaked newsprint until it was like a purée. We added three tablespoons of cornstarch and two cups of water to the newsprint purée, stirring well.

3 We removed some pulp from the bowl with a square piece of window screen as the pulp was rising to the top.

4 We spread the pulp evenly over the window screen and covered it with waxed paper, placing heavy bricks on top as weights.

5 The fibers dried overnight. Finally, we gently peeled the sheets of paper off the screen.

Reflection:

This was one of my favorite Egyptian activities because it was fun, interesting, and I was able to work with my friends. One mistake I made when making the paper was to put too much water in the bowl when soaking the newsprint. I had to start the whole project over the next day.

Frieze of Scenes Depicting

The Life of a Pharaoh

PURPOSE

Life as a pharaoh in Egypt must have been interesting and demanding. The pharaoh was the ruler of the Egyptians and was greatly respected by his people. The Syrians, who lived in a mountainous land northeast of Egypt, were conquered by the great Pharaoh Thutmose III and were often forced to send tribute to Egypt.

WHAT I DID

I designed a frieze that shows different scenes from a typical day in the life of the great Pharaoh Thutmose III. The frieze was drawn on a large roll of shelf paper that was divided into seven different sections. Each section depicted one of the events outlined here. I created the scenes using a combination of crayons and watercolor.

Scene One: This scene shows Pharaoh beginning his day. His servants dress him, and he puts on his "nemes" headdress, a symbol of royalty.

Scene Two: This scene shows Pharaoh performing the ritual of burning incense in the temple as an offering to the god Amon.

Scene Three: This scene shows Pharaoh with his advisors on hand, receiving and reading dispatches that will help him solve the problems of government. He has heard rumors of a revolt among the Syrians.

Scene Four: This scene shows Pharaoh supervising the construction of a pyramid he is building to keep his body safe after death.

Scene Five: This scene shows Pharaoh hunting ducks for his evening meal.

Scene Six: This scene shows Pharaoh receiving guests and gifts at a reception in the palace. He sits with his wife in the audience-hall.

Scene Seven: This is Pharaoh playing a game of "senit" with his daughter.

Reflection:

I didn't do well on this assignment at all because Egyptian figures in paintings are quite different from the figures in the art I know. Egyptian artists drew the shoulders and chest as they would be seen from the front, while arms and legs might be drawn from the side. The head was usually drawn in profile and important people like the Pharaoh were always drawn larger than the other people in the scene. My frieze is now at home on my bedroom wall.

Construction of a
Paddle Doll

PURPOSE

Paddle dolls were popular in Egypt. They were not often used as toys, but as company for the dead. These funny dolls were buried in the tombs of pharaohs and other important people to serve their masters in the afterlife. Paddle dolls were made of wood and had hair made of clay beads attached with twine. They were painted to look like servants such as bakers, farmers, and peasants. They had paddles instead of feet so that they could not run away.

WHAT I DID

I constructed my own paddle doll from a cardboard box. I used black yarn for her hair and dyed pieces of macaroni for the beads. A picture of my paddle doll is drawn here, and the "real thing" is stored in my portfolio file box.

Reflection

This project was easy to do and took me only two days to complete. I did a good job on it. It is one of my favorite pieces in my portfolio.

Two Reviews of

Picture Books about Egypt

TITLE:

Mummies Made in Egypt

AUTHOR AND ILLUSTRATOR:

Aliki

PUBLISHER:

Harper Trophy Publications, 1985

This book explores the mystery of the Egyptian mummy hidden by layers of bandage and covered with priceless jewels. The reader of *Mummies Made in Egypt* will learn the secrets of Egyptians who prepared and wrapped their dead to last forever. Step by step we are taken through the seventy-day process, from the embalmer's slab to the depths of the tomb, where the mummy was sealed away and sent to its life in eternity.

The author begins with a brief account of ancient Egyptian religious beliefs and with sketches showing some of the gods and goddesses. The reasons these gods and goddesses were important to the people are examined. Many artifacts, paintings, and symbols found in the tombs of the mummies are discussed as part of the step-by-step description of the art of mummification.

The illustrations reflect the stiff stance of the Egyptian painting style and Egyptian clothing and jewelry. Warm earth tones are offset with muted blues and greens.

TITLE:

Hieroglyphs from A to Z

AUTHOR AND ILLUSTRATOR:

Peter Der Manuelian

PUBLISHER:

Museum of Fine Arts, Boston, 1991

This book features forty-eight shiny, colorful pages of rhymes that match letters to Egyptian symbols, one letter at a time. The large color hieroglyph on each of the alphabet pages shows a picture of a word that begins with the letter on that page. The hieroglyphs are beautiful reproductions of real ancient carvings and paintings.

At the bottom of each letter page is a smaller hieroglyph in a box, an ancient Egyptian hieroglyph that stands for the sound our English letter makes. All of the drawings are based on actual hieroglyphs that are carved or painted on Egyptian tomb and temple walls, and many of the drawings come from samples on display at the Museum of Fine Arts in Boston.

At the back is a brief history of hieroglyphs and a chart to help the reader learn the hieroglyphs that match our alphabet. The best thing about the book is that it comes with a set of stencils to help the reader write his or her name in hieroglyphs!

Reflection

Both books were interesting and easy to understand because they were written for kids. I liked this assignment because I could learn the ideas on my own, even though studying Egypt is not easy. I did a good job. These are two of my best book reports. Sometimes I wish I could have lived during Egyptian times.

Map of Ancient Egypt

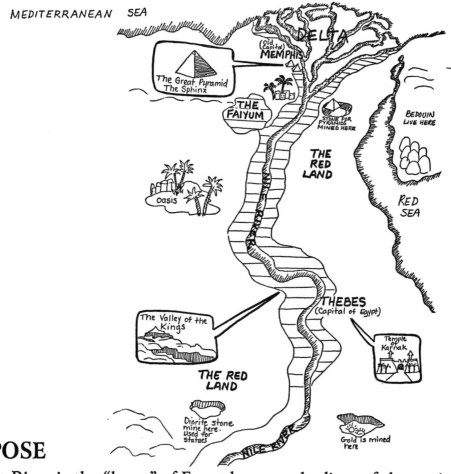

PURPOSE

The Nile River is the "heart" of Egypt because the lives of the ancient Egyptians revolved around it. The Nile River flows more than 4000 miles north across the continent of Africa to the Mediterranean Sea. The Nile is important to the Egyptians because it nourishes the fertile Nile Valley, providing food and water to the people; because people settled on its banks and used the Nile for food, travel, and trade; and because it played a role in their religious beliefs through the important god of the Nile named Hapi.

WHAT I DID

I created a map of ancient Egypt showing its dependence on the Nile River.

> ### Reflection
>
> This is my very best artifact in the portfolio because of its detail and accuracy. As I researched information on the Nile, I wanted to add more descriptions of life along the Nile but ran out of time and room. I would love to take a trip down the Nile today! I wonder if is polluted as are so many of our rivers.

Timeline of Ancient Egypt

PURPOSE

Egypt has a long history of different periods, leaders, wars, and conquerors. A visual timeline helps people to understand the different stages of their history.

WHAT I DID

I read several books on the history of Egypt and have recorded the most important ones below. I constructed a colorful timeline of these dates and corresponding symbols on a long strip of adding machine tape, which is stored in my portfolio file box.

3100 BC	ARCHAIC PERIOD: First period in Egyptian history, unified under first king, Narmer.
2686 BC	OLD KINGDOM: Second period in Egyptian history, when Egypt became a great nation and built the pyramids.
2181 BC	FIRST INTERMEDIATE PERIOD: Unstable period in Egyptian history, when Egypt had five different pharaohs.
2040 BC	MIDDLE KINGDOM: Unified period in Egyptian history for 400 years, until invaded by Hyksos.
1786 BC	SECOND INTERMEDIATE PERIOD: Period in Egyptian history when ruled by Hyksos.
1570 BC	NEW KINGDOM: Golden age period in Egyptian history, which included reigns of Amenhotep IV, Tutankhamon, Ramses II, and Ramses III.
1085 BC	THIRD INTERMEDIATE PERIOD: Period in Egyptian history when Egypt was divided and weak, and ruled by Libyan and Nubian kings.
c. 751 BC	LATER PERIOD: Period in Egyptian history when constantly invaded by Assyrians and Persians.
333–30 BC	PTOLEMAIC PERIOD: Period in Egyptian history when Alexander the Great conquered Egypt and ended with the Roman conquest.

Reflection

I don't think my timeline was very good because I found all of these dates and periods hard to understand and boring to read about. I included this artifact in my portfolio because it was one of my worst pieces of work.

My Portfolio Rubric/Conference Questions

RATING SCALE

1 = I could have done better   2 = I did a good job   3 = I did a terrific job

ARTIFACTS

1. Organization and completeness of portfolio ☐ 1 ☐ 2 ☐ 3

2. Quality of artifacts selected ☐ 1 ☐ 2 ☐ 3

3. Creativity shown in work ☐ 1 ☐ 2 ☐ 3

4. Correctness of work (grammar, spelling, sentence structure, neatness, punctuation, etc.) ☐ 1 ☐ 2 ☐ 3

5. Evidence of learning concepts and/or applying skills ☐ 1 ☐ 2 ☐ 3

6. Reflection process ☐ 1 ☐ 2 ☐ 3

7. Evidence of enthusiasm and interest in assignments ☐ 1 ☐ 2 ☐ 3

8. Oral presentation of portfolio ☐ 1 ☐ 2 ☐ 3

QUESTIONS I WISH OTHERS WOULD ASK ME ABOUT MY PORTFOLIO

1. What was your favorite artifact and why?

2. What are the three most interesting things you learned about ancient Egypt?

3. What was your hardest task during this unit of study?

4. If you had lived during the ancient Egyptian period of history, would you rather have been a scribe, a warrior, a peasant, a Pharaoh, a wealthy landowner, or a navigator of the Nile? Give reasons for your answer.

GRADING SCALE
22–24 Points = A
18–21 Points = B
14–17 Points = C
10–13 Points = D
Under 10 Points = Unacceptable

My Personal Comments

I enjoyed this unit immensely and had a hard time deciding what artifacts to include in my portfolio. The hardest things for me in completing my work for this project were: (1) Understanding some of the Egyptian terms and explanations because they were so different; (2) Editing my work for improving both grammar and expression of ideas; and (3) Presenting the contents of this portfolio to the class because I don't like to speak in front of groups!

A Very Practical Appendix

Ten High-interest Strategies/Activities to Integrate Science into Social Studies

1 **Use the scientific method to test a hypothesis.**

Example: Create a hypothesis to serve as the basis for exploration of the factors most responsible for getting out the vote on election day.

2 **Examine the concepts of systems and ecosystems.**

Example: Explain what is meant by the ecosystem of a city and how the decay of many American cities is related to the concept of an ecosystem. Compare this to an ecosystem found in nature.

Example: Describe how the systems of a city are like the systems of the human body. Consider the transportation system, communication systems, economic system, political system, and the social systems of a community.

3 **Identify cause and effect situations.**

Example: Determine the causes and effects of the American Civil War on the attitudes and lifestyles of people from both the North and the South.

4 **Study the impact of weather and natural disasters.**

Example: Give examples of how the weather in a given geographic area determines how people live and what people do.

Example: Draw a diagram to show how a natural disaster such as an earthquake in Japan or a hurricane in Florida can have an impact on the local economy.

5 **Experiment with cycles and chain reactions.**

Example: Show how the passage of a law such as one that requires labels on food products can cause a chain reaction of responses by both manufacturers and consumers.

Example: Show how the recycling of used products can save natural resources.

6 **Use the biomes as springboards for geography.**

Example: Construct a chart to show the similarities and differences in the lifestyles of people who live in each of these settings: grasslands, deserts, tundra, deciduous forests, coniferous forests, and rainforests.

7 **Use the earth and the moon to explain time and the calendar.**

Example: Using the globe, show how the rotation of the earth affects the tides, the seasons, and the time in different parts of the world.

8 **Use principles of energy, motion, and work to explain advances in technology.**

Example: Write a short report showing how an invention of your choice reduces the amount of work and energy required to do a complex job.

9 **Examine ways that plant and animal life affect food sources.**

Example: Do some research to find out how a society like Japan or China develops eating habits and food sources that are different from those in a society like the United States.

10 **Examine ways that principles of light and sound are used to improve technology.**

Example: Determine ways that science has improved our ability to communicate with one another. Consider such inventions as the telephone, the telegraph, the television, the computer, the camcorder, and the tape player.

Ten High-interest Strategies/Activities to Integrate Math into Social Studies

1 **Use Venn Diagrams to compare and contrast people, places, events.**

Example: Compare and contrast the New England colonies of Massachusetts (Plymouth), Rhode Island (Providence), and Connecticut (Hartford), using the following variables: year founded, founder, chief crops of trade, government, and religion.

2 **Construct line graphs, bar graphs, circle graphs, and pictographs.**

Example: Construct a line graph to show the immigration pattern for Florida during the last ten years.

3 **Create word or story problems.**

Example: Did you know that 20 to 50 inches of dry, powdery snow when melted yields just one inch of water? How much snow in the coldest parts of Russia would be needed to generate 12 inches of water according to this formula?

4 **Use money and monetary systems of the United States and other countries.**

Example: Using a currency conversion chart from your local newspaper, convert $10.00 in U.S. dollars to the foreign currency in dollars for Japan, France, and Mexico. Which country would give you the greatest value if you were to visit that country on a vacation?

5 **Construct flow charts or diagrams to show processes for making or doing something.**

Example: Construct a diagram to show how a bill becomes a law.

6 **Discover the elements of geometry in different cultures by examining their art, architecture, monuments, artifacts, homes, and lifestyles.**

Example: Do some research to find out the role that geometry played in the construction of the Pyramids of Egypt, the Great Wall of China, the Eiffel Tower of Paris, and the Golden Gate Bridge of San Francisco.

7 **Conduct individual or group surveys and show results in chart form.**

Example: Take a survey of the students in your class to determine their ancestries. Show your results in chart form.

8 **Use number codes or ancient number systems to rewrite math problems or social studies facts.**

Example: Use a number code to write three key facts about the American Revolution. See if a friend can decipher your code and uncover your facts.

Example: Use the number symbols of the Egyptians to rewrite one of your math problems from today's math class.

9 **Construct timelines to establish the chronology of important events.**

Example: Make a timeline to show the most significant events in the life of a famous explorer, inventor, or political leader.

10 **Use linear measures to determine distances on a map.**

Example: Use the mileage scale on the U.S. map to determine the best route to take when driving from Detroit, Michigan, to Toronto, Canada.

Ten High-interest Strategies/Activities to Integrate Language Arts into Social Studies

1 **Write reports or speeches and give them orally.**

Example: Prepare a short "speech to inform" that explains both the causes and results of the Spanish-American War.

2 **Express information through various forms of poetry.**

Example: Describe your geographical setting using these five poetry forms: haiku, diamante, free verse, concrete, and acrostic. Title your work "Five Ways to Look at a Landform."

3 **Use diaries or learning logs to record feelings, ideas, reflections, and observations.**

Example: After reading *The Diary of Anne Frank*, create a series of diary entries for another victim of prejudice such as a slave during Civil War times or a Vietnamese orphan during the war in Vietnam.

Example: Keep a learning log to record your feelings, reactions, and ideas about the Classsic Period of Mayan History as you complete your textbook chapter and outside readings.

4 **Use children's literature and picture books.**

Example: Collect a series of picture books about people from foreign lands. Read the books and write a synopsis for each one. Determine what makes these books both appealing and informative.

5 **Read folktales, legends, myths, and tall tales.**

Example: Select a Greek or Roman mythological character to study and prepare a short picture essay that tells something about him or her.

6 **Read biographies of famous leaders, scientists, explorers, inventors, authors, artists, mathematicians, etc.**

Example: Develop an outline about the person whose biography you chose to read. Use this outline to share information about your person with members of your cooperative reading group.

7 Use the dictionary as a tool for acquiring information.

Example: Use the dictionary to define these terms related to our study of geography: island, peninsula, and isthmus.

Example: Use the dictionary to help you determine the origins of these terms associated with the computer: virus, boot up, debug, and terminal.

8 Compose original short stories.

Example: Choose one of the following topics to write an original story related to our study of consumer economics.

- A Bargain That Cost Me Money
- There's No Such Thing as a Free Lunch
- My Perfect Purchase
- To Buy or Not to Buy, That Is the Question!
- Buyer Beware

9 Write and send friendly or business letters.

Example: Choose one piece of correspondence from your junk mail collection, and respond to the business who sent it, expressing your thoughts and reactions to the contents of their mail.

Example: Send a friendly letter to the owner of your favorite store or retail outlet to tell him or her why you patronize the business.

10 Incorporate grammar into tasks.

Example: Browse through your textbook (or a newspaper or news magazine) and select a picture showing a current event of special interest to you. Write sentences related to the content of the picture: a declarative sentence, an interrogative sentence, an exclamatory sentence, and a sentence that gives a command.

Example: Make a list of common nouns, proper nouns, and verbs that describe or explain the Civil Rights movement.

Topics for Student Reports

CIVICS AND POLITICAL SCIENCE

Branches of Government

Citizenship

Civil Rights

Constitution and Bill of Rights

Declaration of Independence

Famous Criminals, Court Cases, and Trials

Justice

Legal System and Laws

Mayflower Compact

Monroe Doctrine

Patriotism

Political Parties

Royalty

Suffrage

Unions

U.S. Presidents

Voting/Electoral College

ECONOMICS

Advertising

Allowances

Banking

Bargains and Sales

Consumer Choices and Spending

Consumers and Producers/Products and Services/Supply and Demand

Entrepreneurship

Interest and Savings

Investments and Stock Market

Money

Trade Agreements and Exports

Types of Businesses

Types of Credit

Warranties

GEOGRAPHY

Beauty Spots

Canals and Locks

Caves and Canyons

Cities and Towns

Countries or Continents

Earth's Regions/Biomes

Ecology

Islands and Peninsulas

Landform

Maps and Globes

Migrations

Mountain Ranges

Natural Disasters

Natural Resources

Oceans, Lakes, and Rivers

Rain Forests

Spaces and Places

HISTORY

American Revolution

Ancient Civilizations

Assassins and Traitors

Aztec

Catacombs

Civil War

Colonies

Crusades

Diaries, Letters, and Journals

Diseases: Black Death

Empires

Explorers

Famous Men and Famous Women

Famous Speeches and Debates

Futuristics

Gods and Kings

Great Depression

Great Wall of China

Historical Chronologies

Historical Facts and Opinions

Historical Landmarks

Historical Period: Renaissance

Historical Research

History through the Cemeteries

Ideas and Images

Ideologies

International Relations

Inventions and Discoveries

Lifestyles

Middle Ages

Nobel Prize

Peace Corps

People, Places, and Things of History

Pirates and Pioneers

Pony Express

Presidents

Revolutions and Rebellions

Transportation

United Nations

U.S. or World History Benchmarks

Wars and Battles

World Leaders

SOCIOLOGY /ANTHROPOLOGY

Age and Gender Groups

Anthropology

Arts/Architecture/Music/Theater

Beliefs

Careers and World of Work

Communication

Conflicts

Cultures

Customs, Fads, Fashions

Famous Bridges and Buildings

Flags

Foreign Languages

Holidays and Celebrations

Human Behavior

Legends

Lifestyles

Networks

Stereotypes and Prejudices

Uniforms, Headwear, and Footgear

Values and Ethics

151

Interdisciplinary Unit in Social Studies

Title: _____

Topic (or Theme): _____

- Purpose

- Objectives

- Glossary

- Introductory Activity

- Activities or Projects in Related Content Areas
  - MATH

  - SCIENCE

  - LANGUAGE ARTS

  - ENRICHMENT OR EXPLORATORY

- Homework or Independent Study Projects

- Cooperative Learning Activity

- Culminating Activity

- Assessment

Integrating Social Studies to Accommodate Multiple Intelligences

Social Studies Theme: _____

	Science	Math	Language Arts
VERBAL/ LINGUISTIC			
LOGICAL/ MATHEMATICAL			
VISUAL/SPATIAL			
BODY/ KINESTHETIC			
MUSICAL/ RHYTHMICAL			
INTERPERSONAL			
INTRAPERSONAL			

NOTE: Not every square need be filled in for every topic. Just make sure there is a good content balance in each unit.

Integrating Social Studies to Accommodate Williams' Taxonomy

Social Studies Theme: _____

	Science	Math	Language Arts
FLUENCY			
FLEXIBILITY			
ORIGINALITY			
ELABORATION			
RISK TAKING			
COMPLEXITY			
CURIOSITY			
IMAGINATION			

NOTE: Not every square need be filled in for every topic. Just make sure there is a good content balance in each unit.

Teacher Checklist to Aid in the Promotion of Journal Writing in the Social Studies Classroom

Purposes

How do you present the purposes of a journal to your students when you are making journal assignments?

A journal is a . . .

a. _____ sourcebook/collection of ideas, thoughts, and opinions.

b. _____ place to write first drafts/ outlines of papers and projects.

c. _____ place to record observations of and/or questions about something read, written, or discussed.

d. _____ recordkeeping tool to use to keep track of what and how much was read/researched on a topic.

e. _____ place in which to write personal reactions or responses to a textbook assignment, group discussion, research finding, or audiovisual resource.

f. _____ reference file to help a student monitor individual growth or progress in a given area.

g. _____ way for students to "dialogue" in written form with peers and teachers.

h. _____ place for a student to write about topics that he or she has chosen.

1. _____ place for reflections on and paraphrases of material learned.

Formats

Which of the following journal formats is most appealing to you?

a. _____ special notebooks

b. _____ segments of audiotapes

c. _____ file cards

d. _____ handmade diaries

Writing Time

Which of the following time options is most practical for you?

a. _____ daily for five minutes

b. _____ semi-weekly for ten minutes

c. _____ weekly for fifteen minutes

d. _____ when needed

Student Feedback

Which of these formal/informal methods makes most sense to you?

a. _____ student sharing of journal entries with peers

b. _____ reading journal entries aloud to class on a volunteer basis

c. _____ using journals for "conferencing"

d. _____ taking journal entries home to share with parents/guardians

e. _____ analyzing and answering one's own journal entry one or more days after entry was recorded to acknowledge personal changes in perspective

Annotated Bibliography

An annotated bibliography of Incentive Publications titles selected to provide additional help for integrating instruction in social studies

Breeden, Terri. *Cooperative Learning Companion.* Nashville, TN: Incentive Publications, 1992. *(Grades 5-8)*
Creative teaching aids include charts, forms, and posters. Comprehensive instructions tell how to set up an effective cooperative classroom environment.

Breeden, Terri and Emalie Egan. *Strategies and Activities to Raise Achievement.* Nashville, TN: Incentive Publications, 1995. *(Grades 4-8)*
A comprehensive manual containing high-interest activities and esteem-building exercises designed to motivate students to become more effective test-takers and successful lifelong learners.

Cook, Shirley. *180 Days Around the World.* Nashville, TN: Incentive Publications, 1993. *(Grades 4-8)*
Global challenges that send students on an adventure around the world, providing unique opportunities to discuss, research, think, imagine, and explore.

Farnette, Cherrie, Imogene Forte, and Barbara Loss. *I've Got Me and I'm Glad, Revised Edition.* Nashville, TN: Incentive Publications, 1989. *(Grades 4-7)*
A self-awareness resource with high-interest reproducible activities designed to help kids identify their strengths and weaknesses and establish short- and long-range goals.

—. *People Need Each Other, Revised Edition.* Nashville, TN: Incentive Publications, 1989. *(Grades 4-7)*
These social awareness activities were designed to build student understanding of family, peers, and the community by encouraging the use of effective communication skills.

Forte, Imogene. *One Nation, 50 States.* Nashville, TN: Incentive Publication, 1993. *(Grades 4-7)*
Fifty interdisciplinary units include high-interest activities, extended learning projects, and lessons to enhance higher-level thinking skills. Everything needed for the activities and lessons is provided in the pages of this creative study of the United States.

—. *Writing Survival Skills for the Middle Grades.* Nashville, TN: Incentive Publications, 1991. *(Grades 5-8)*
Test-taking, resumes, business letters, and job applications are just a few of the topics covered in this essential writing skills handbook.

Forte, Imogene and Sandra Schurr. *The Cooperative Learning Guide and Planning Pak for Middle Grades.* Nashville, TN: Incentive Publications, 1992. *(Grades 5-8)*
A collection of high-interest thematic units, thematic thinking skills projects, and thematic poster projects. Includes reference skills sharpeners and much more.

—. *The Definitive Middle School Guide: A Handbook for Success.* Nashville, TN: Incentive Publications, 1993. *(Grades 5-8)*
This comprehensive, research-based manual provides the perfect overview for educators and administrators who are determined to establish a school environment that stimulates and motivates the Middle Grade student in the learning process.

—. *Interdisciplinary Units and Projects for Thematic Instruction for Middle Grade Success.* Nashville, TN: Incentive Publications, 1994. *(Grades 5-8)*
A jumbo-sized collection of thematic-based interdisciplinary activities and assignments that was created to spark interest, encourage communication, and promote problem solving as well as decision making.

—. *Making Portfolios, Products, and Performances Meaningful and Manageable for Students and Teachers.* Nashville, TN: Incentive Publications, 1995. *(Grades 4-8)*
Filled with valuable information and specific suggestions for incorporating authentic assessment techniques that help students enjoy a more active role in the evaluation process. Includes a convenient pull-out Graphic Organizer with creative ideas for integrating content instruction and appraising student understanding.

—. *Middle Grades Advisee/Advisor Program.* Nashville, TN: Incentive Publications, 1991. *(Grades 5-8)*
A comprehensive program dedicated to meeting the needs and confronting the challenges of today's young adolescent students. A flexible, manageable curriculum, available at three different levels, that contains both a teacher's guide and over 300 reproducible activities on essential topics.

—. *Tools, Treasures, and Measures for Middle Grade Success.* Nashville, TN: Incentive Publications, 1994. *(Grades 5-8)*
This practical resource offers a wide assortment of teaching essentials, from ready-to-use lesson plans and student assignments to valuable lists and assessment tools.

Frender, Gloria. *Learning to Learn.* Nashville, TN: Incentive Publications, 1990. *(All grades)*
Creative ideas, practical suggestions, and "hands on" materials to help students acquire organizational, study, test-taking, and problem-solving skills needed to become lifelong effective learners.

Graham, Leland and Darriel Ledbetter. *How to Write a Great Research Paper.* Nashville, TN: Incentive Publications, 1994. *(Grades 5-8)*
Mini-lessons help students choose and narrow topics, locate information, take notes, organize an outline, develop a rough draft, document sources, as well as write, revise, and evaluate their final papers.

Philpot, Jan and Ed. *Partners in Learning and Growing: Linking the Home, School, and Community through Curriculum-based Programs.* Nashville, TN: Incentive Publications, 1994. *(Grades 5-8)*
Original programs designed to give a teacher or an entire school a year-long plan for fostering community and parental involvement.

U. S. Social Studies YELLOW PAGES for Students and Teachers, compiled by Kathy LaMorte and Sharen Lewis. Nashville, TN: Incentive Publications, 1993. *(Grades 2-8)*
Contains valuable facts, lists, charts, and definitions related to U. S. exploration, historic sites, famous Americans, maps, folklore, and more.

World Social Studies YELLOW PAGES for Students and Teachers, compiled by Kathy LaMorte and Sharen Lewis. Nashville, TN: Incentive Publications, 1993. *(Grades 2-8)*
A collection of facts, charts, and lists on the topics of world civilization, exploration, geographical regions, time zones, population, and more.

Index

Index entries in bold type are titles of student activities.